100 BEST
NEW ZEALAND
NATIVE PLANTS
FOR GARDENS

100 BEST
NEW ZEALAND
NATIVE PLANTS
FOR GARDENS

Fiona Eadie

GODWIT

DEDICATION

I would like to dedicate this book to my mother, Meriel, for whom gardening is almost as important as breathing. As a child I remember that if she was tired or stressed, she used to go out and garden and somehow come back rejuvenated. She passed this love of gardening and plants on to her children.

ACKNOWLEDGEMENTS

I could try to list all those people through my life who have shared their knowledge with me but I would not know where to begin, so I have decided to mention only those people who have helped me with this book.

Firstly, and most importantly, I would like to thank Jane Connor of Random House for her patience and enthusiasm for this book and for giving me the necessary push to get something down on paper; without her this would never have happened. I would also like to thank Geoff Davidson, the owner of Oratia Native Plant Nursery, who not only read through the early drafts but also freely shared his horticultural and botanical knowledge to me over the years I worked there. John Wyse, the nursery's plant health expert, has provided invaluable assistance with the pests and problems of the various species. I would also like to acknowledge Ewen Cameron, Curator of Botany at the Auckland Museum, for his patience with me, since my early Forest Service days, in identifying plant specimens and answering my questions. Finally, I would like to thank my partner, Mick, for his support not only with this book but with everything else.

All photographs in this book are by Yvonne Cave, with the exception of the following: page 117 (bottom), Gil Hanly; pages 77 (4), 78, 80, 84 (bottom), 88, Jack Hobbs; pages 21 (top right and bottom), 22, 24, 29, 35, 39, 47, 53, 54, 55, 58, 101 (middle and bottom), 109, 116, 118, 120 (bottom), 124, 127, 138 (top), 191 (2), Rob Lucas.

A GODWIT BOOK
published by
Random House New Zealand
18 Poland Road, Glenfield, Auckland, New Zealand
www.randomhouse.co.nz

First published 2001

ISBN 1 86962 069 0

Design and production: Kate Greenaway
Cover illustration: *Arthropodium cirratum*, rengarenga (Rob Lucas)
Printed in Hong Kong

CONTENTS

INTRODUCTION

Plants have always been a part of my life in one way or another, from weeding gardens as a child to studying botany at university and, more recently, managing a native plant nursery. Over the years I have come to appreciate the variety and splendour of New Zealand's native plants, from the large almost god-like kauri to the low sprawling groundcovers, and all forms in between. All have a place in the natural environment, and most also have a place in the garden. By mixing and matching, an infinite variety of plant associations and landscapes can be created for any set of climatic and environmental conditions.

When deciding on the 100 native plants to include in this book, I first looked at the major groupings familiar to most gardeners: trees, shrubs, herbaceous plants and grasses, groundcovers, and, of course, ferns and vines. Within each of these categories I chose species that have proved themselves in cultivation and are relatively hardy through much of New Zealand, if grown in the correct environment. I also tried to cover a range of textures and colours while remembering the importance of availability. Native plants are generally more widely available in North Island nurseries and garden centres; in the south you may have to be a little more diligent in your searching, but you will find all of the plants included here.

It is difficult to write a book that applies to gardeners the length and breadth of the country. New Zealand covers a huge range in latitude, from the cool temperate climate of the deep south to the almost tropical conditions of the far north, and all possible combinations of climatic conditions in between. Plants do not necessarily require the same conditions at one end of the country as they do at the other, especially in cultivation. In the north high temperatures combined with high humidity create a raft of problems for many species, both above and below ground. A majority of these problems are fungal, but insect damage and other plant-related diseases also tend to be more severe. For example *Carex buchananii* and *Pseudopanax arboreus* can tolerate quite damp soils in cooler areas but require dry free-draining soils or a cool root run in warmer areas; suitable conditions can often be created by using other plants as groundcovers or providing large rocks.

I hope that this book will provide an introduction to the huge and sometimes daunting array of native plants that are available, and that it will help you understand the plants themselves, what their requirements are, how to get the best out of them, and how to use them effectively in a garden.

COMMON MISCONCEPTIONS ABOUT NATIVE PLANTS

Before going any further we should clear up a few common misconceptions about native plants:

• *Plants that occur in extreme conditions in the wild, eg very dry, very wet or very windy, actually grow best in such conditions.*

The truth is that while the vast majority of plants *tolerate* and compete well against other species in such extremes, they will grow more vigorously if provided with 'average' growing conditions.

• *Native plants do not need feeding or looking after because they naturally occur here.*

Native plants are no different from any other plant, strangely enough. They will survive without compost, mulch or other forms of feeding but the health and vigour of the plant will be entirely dependent on the make-up and nutrients of your particular soil. The more care and attention you give plants, the better they will grow. Mulch and /or compost provide the plant with food over a period of time while improving the soil structure. Organic matter improves the soil's water-holding capabilities in the summer and drainage in the winter, and provides food for worms and other decomposers that subsequently pass it on to the plant and aerate the soil.

• *Native plants do not need watering because they naturally occur here.*

Providing a plant with the right watering regime is as important as feeding it. If a plant is looking ill, first check whether it is too wet or too dry. For the preferred conditions, check the summary at the end of each description.

To minimise watering, plant in autumn when the plant has a chance to stabilise in the ground before the spring growth begins. In warmer northern areas the optimum time to plant is once the ground becomes wet in April. By planting at this time you can also take advantage of the autumn growing season, which in some areas can be as pronounced as spring.

• *Native plants are slow growing.*

As with all plants, some natives are slow and some are comparatively vigorous. The main thing to remember is provide your plant with the best growing conditions possible.

A GOLDEN RULE: *Plant the right plants in the right places*
If your garden is dry, plant dry-loving plants; if it is damp, plant damp-loving, and if it has areas of both, as is so often the case, plant species that will tolerate these conditions. By doing this you are minimising the effort that you need to put in, not to mention the amount of water— and you can go on holiday in the middle of summer and not have to worry about your plants!

However, you can modify your growing conditions. If you want to plant a moderately dry-loving species in a flat damp site, plant it above the soil level; by digging a hole you will create a bucket. Cover the area where you want to plant with a few centimetres of free-draining fertile mix (eg a well-matured compost and topsoil mix). Prepare the plant (ensuring the roots are not encircling the main root ball) and place it on the new mix. Cover the roots of the plant with the same mix, forming a mound in the process. Taper the mix to ground level, ensuring that the sides are not too steep. Over the years the plant will require new applications of compost and food to sustain growth, just as with any other plant.

If you want to plant a dry-loving plant on a sloped site, you can either cut a wedge into the side of the slope or cut a drainage trench into the hole that you dig. Both methods will allow water to drain out easily and hence prevent waterlogging of the soil. Provide good free-draining mix around the plant.

If you want to retain water on a dry site, you will need to improve the water-holding capacity of the substrate, which is most easily done by adding organic matter. Peat is often used but it is not a renewable resource and is acidic, hence tying up nutrients in the soil. I prefer compost, which should be mixed in with the soil and watered well before planting. Spread a good thick layer of mulch around the plant, leaving a space around the base of each plant, and water well again. It is essential that you plant in autumn through to early spring in such areas, especially if you do not wish to irrigate. If irrigation is a necessity for the first couple of years of establishment, make sure you water for a long period of time so that the lower soil strata become saturated. The motto is more water less often! Walking around with a hose each evening will tend to bring the plant's roots to the surface where they will be a lot more susceptible to drying out.

The checklists that appear with each entry were intended as a quick summary to enable you to see if you have the right conditions for the species that you are thinking of growing. The height, or range, given is an average; in harsh conditions the plant will be shorter and in an ideal environment the plant may be taller. Shade will usually increase the height of a plant. For the environmental conditions, the term 'tolerate' is used where plants can withstand a particular situation but will not grow well if the conditions are extreme. 'Hardy' has been used when the species will handle extremes; no plants thrive in such conditions and their growth rates will be slower.

My scientific background makes me want to be as accurate as possible in my terminology. However, my more recent nursery background and appreciation of what terms people recognise has meant that I have used a few terms more loosely than is scientifically accurate. For example, the word 'grasses' has been used very loosely and covers not only true grasses like *Festuca coxii* but also *Carex* species, which are more correctly sedges. With tree ferns the term 'trunk' has been used where caudex is more accurate, but the former is by far the more widely understood.

But enough of this talk and on to the real work of gardening with our own native plants, not someone else's. People overseas recognise our foodstuffs, our fashion, our boat-building capabilities and even our plants. It is time that we too all celebrated their diversity and uniqueness by using them in our gardens. Onwards!

Fiona Eadie
2001

Titoki is one of New Zealand's classic shade trees and in many northern cities and towns is a common street tree. It is naturally a single-leader tree with a clear trunk and a full, slightly spreading canopy. The attractive glossy dark green leaves are made up of a number of serrated leaflets, the new growth of which can have a lovely pink hue. Titoki flowers occur on stalked flowerheads up to 30 cm long in late spring/early summer. The major feature, however, is the fruit, which occur within quite woody capsules covered in a rusty brown tomentum, attractive in their own right. The fruit can take up to a year to mature but when the capsules split the bright red fruit is displayed with the shiny black seed exposed, like an eye-ball in a red eye. The birds love these fruit.

Titoki is naturally found from North Cape to Banks Peninsula on the east coast and to further south on the west. It occurs in lowland forest, especially on alluvial plains.

Black seed and bright red fruit of titoki

LIKES AND DISLIKES: Titoki can tolerate light frosts although the outermost foliage may become burnt. It prefers a rich free-draining soil and will not tolerate extremes of soil moisture. If planted in a windy position, expect some windburn and stunted growth. Although tolerant of light shade, titoki prefers full sun.

PESTS AND PROBLEMS: A disease is becoming more common in the north of New Zealand, the cause of which is uncertain. The new growth dies off, leaving apparently bare stalks. The plant will eventually resprout on the good wood but this does take time. Each time it occurs it saps the plant of energy and stunts the plant. Until it is identified, there are no suggested remedies.

CARE AND MAINTENANCE: Titoki requires little attention after planting. Mulching and/or composting will help provide nutrients and maintain soil moisture through the summer months; do keep both well away from the trunk of the tree.

Seed is the normal means of propagation and they germinate readily.

LANDSCAPING SUGGESTIONS: Titoki's classic shape makes it ideal as a specimen tree. Once established it can be underplanted or the ground simply paved or grassed. If underplanting,

species like rengarenga, *Libertia*, *Coprosma rhamnoides*, *Astelia* and *Hebe diosmifolia* could be used, with *Fuchsia procumbens* as a groundcover. Although titoki can be a spreading tree, it can be part of a mixed planting where it will spread to fit the available space. If a large area is to be planted, rimu, *Hoheria sexstylosa*, silver beech, taraire and maire could be planted with it. A grove of titoki can look good, especially if simply underplanted, showing off the pillar-like trunks to their full beauty.

- Tree 6 m+ tall
- Full sun to semi-shade
- Tolerates some dryness
- Wet intolerant
- Prefers sheltered conditions
- Tolerates light frosts

Top: Titoki foliage
Above: A mature tree showing the clear trunk and rounded head

Taraire is one of the larger broad-leaved plants in the forest, at 20 m or more tall. However, in the garden situation it grows to 6–9 m. From seedling to adult, taraire is aesthetically pleasing. For many years of its life it has a classic pyramidal shape with striking beech-like tiers of branches, although as the leaves are larger these tiers are not always as pronounced as in the beech. It is usually a single-leader tree but if the primary bud, on the tip, becomes damaged it will become a multi-leader tree. (See below in CARE AND MAINTENANCE to right this if it is not the desired form.) Over the years the form of the tree will slowly change to a clear trunk with a spreading canopy. Taraire is not fast growing so will take many years to transform into this

Taraire foliage with ripe purple fruit

habit. The leaves are 10 cm long x 4 cm wide, a dark olive-green colour, which tones with the red/brown to bronze tomentum of the new growth. The flowers are of little significance but the large purple fruit that form afterwards provide plenty of food for pigeons.

Taraire is found only in the north of the North Island, to Kawhia on the west and East Cape on the east. It occurs in coastal to lowland forest.

LIKES AND DISLIKES: Taraire is an easy species to grow. It tolerates shade but will be very spindly, preferring full sun or light shade. It prefers a free-draining soil and can be susceptible to *Phytophthora* if the soil is too wet. Taraire will tolerate very dry conditions as long as it has a cool root run; in sunny conditions this can be provided by planting around the base of the tree or using large rocks. In very exposed situations the leaves can become wind burnt and it's advisable to provide protection for the first few years, leaving it to outgrow the wind break at its own pace. Unfortunately taraire will tolerate only light frosts.

PESTS AND PROBLEMS: If taraire becomes very stressed, it becomes susceptible to thrips, a sucking insect that feeds on chlorophyll. This can be dealt with by spraying with an insecticide, or by alleviating the stress and allowing the plant to grow out of the thrips problem; thrips very rarely kills a plant. Do not allow the soil to become waterlogged and plant where frost will not be a problem.

CARE AND MAINTENANCE: If the main growing tip becomes damaged the tree will become multi-leadered. *FACT-TIME: The terminal or main bud of a normally single-leader tree releases hormones that inhibit the development of the lateral or side branches. If this bud dies, the hormonal control disappears and without it the lateral branches will initially speed up their growth. To allow a new shoot that forms at the tip to dominate, take the tips out of the lateral branches.* To return the tree to a single-leader form, choose the strongest of the new upright shoots and prune out any others. If any of the side shoots still look out of proportion, just prune them back. If the tip remains alive, which it will unless there is frost, drought or physical damage, taraire can be maintenance free apart from mulching.

Seed is the normal form of propagation and germinates moderately quickly.

LANDSCAPING SUGGESTIONS: Taraire is a reasonably large tree and not ideal for a very small inner-city garden, unless, of course, it is used as a centrepiece. With its classic shape, foliage colour, contrasting new shoots and large purple fruit for the birds, what more could you want from a specimen tree? If used as a feature plant in a garden, it could be planted with *Muehlenbeckia astonii*, *Astelia banksii*, *Hebe speciosa*, *Libertia* and *Brachyglottis* species, with *Helichrysum bellidioides* on the edge. In a large mixed planting taraire could be planted with northern rata (remembering that this is slow growing), *Nestegis montana*, karaka, kanuka and rewarewa.

- Large tree 6–9 m tall
- Full sun to shade
- Dry tolerant
- Wind tolerant
- Tolerates light frosts

Putaputaweta is yet another New Zealand native with separate juvenile and adult habits. The juvenile plant is almost divaricating but not quite. The fine branches, extending from the straight main trunk, zigzag very regularly and create quite a tangled appearance. The soft leaves are mottled, with fine serrated edges. As the tree matures the branches straighten out and the leaves become larger (5 cm long x 2–3 cm wide), thicker and glossier. The serrations also become less pronounced and the leaves become darker in colour, though still mottled, hence the name marble leaf. If left to develop naturally in a moist situation, putaputaweta will form a clear single-trunked tree of about 5 m with a broad rounded head. The flowers, which form in late spring through to early summer, are white and although small (5–6 mm), are very prominent. There is also a prostrate form (1 m) of putaputaweta in production. It has the same requirements and, as it is cutting grown from an adult plant, it flowers immediately.

Putaputaweta occurs throughout New Zealand from coastal to montane forests and along streamsides.

LIKES AND DISLIKES: Putaputaweta must have moisture all year round, especially as a juvenile plant. The soft leaves will shrivel as soon as the moisture levels become too low. Soak well and there will be no lasting damage, although in the short term you may lose most of the leaves and any soft new growth; the plant will regrow once it has recovered from the stress. As it is a dry-

Putaputaweta flowers and foliage

intolerant species it is better in a sheltered position where there is minimal effect of drying winds. It will tolerate shade and full sun, and is frost hardy.

PESTS AND PROBLEMS:
Borer can be a problem and will be apparent by the presence of sawdust. If possible, remove infected material. If not, inject the holes with insecticide.

CARE AND
MAINTENANCE:
Putaputaweta does not respond quickly to pruning, which should be borne in mind if undertaking some reshaping. If perchance it loses its tip, possibly through drought, a strong shoot can be chosen from the new shoots that have formed and the weaker ones can be cut away. To prevent drying out in marginal situations, mulch and/or compost every year, remembering to keep this well away from the trunk of the tree.

A juvenile putaputaweta changing into adult foliage

Propagation is by both seed and cuttings, although seed is by far the easier.

LANDSCAPING SUGGESTIONS: The limitations with putaputaweta are its moisture requirements so rather than having to put in an irrigation system, plant it in the right place. If you do not have the right position, don't plant it at all. In the proper place it can look stunning, both in its juvenile and its adult habit. Once a tree has established it can be underplanted with ferns and native grasses. If planting with other trees in a moist gully or around a pond, try mixing it with cabbage trees, manuka, makomako and tree ferns, with swards of *Carex secta* and flaxes.

- 5 m + tall
- 3-4 m wide
- Full sun to shade
- Requires damp conditions
- Frost hardy

Cabbage trees are an integral part of New Zealand's landscape, both physically and emotionally. They are sculptural and architectural in their form, and fast growing, attaining a height of 5–10 m.

The narrowness of form of a pure ti-kouka allows it to fit into the smallest of sites. If undamaged, the tree will not branch until after its first flowering, when it will assume the more classic cabbage tree form.

Tufts of green leaves up to 1 m long form at the end of each branch. The old leaves tend to remain attached for a long period, often hanging like a brown grass skirt around the base of the erect green living leaves.

Large panicles of cream-coloured flowers open from late spring through to early

A grove of ti-kouka showing clear single trunks

summer and are an attractive addition to an already outstanding plant. What's more, the flowers have a delightful honey fragrance that on still warm days and nights can be quite consuming. Maori have the belief that if cabbage trees flower profusely a hot summer will follow.

Cordyline australis occurs naturally on open ground in all but the very driest and coldest of sites from one end of the country to the other.

LIKES AND DISLIKES: There are very few situations that cabbage trees cannot tolerate. If the conditions are excessively dry, the plant may need water to become established, and in areas with excessively low winter temperatures some frost protection would be advisable for the first few years. *Cordyline australis* is more suited to open sunny sites but will tolerate some shade.

PESTS AND PROBLEMS: Many people are scared to plant a cabbage tree in their garden for fear that it will fall prey to the unknown 'cabbage tree disease' that spread rapidly through New

Zealand in the 1980s and 1990s. Very little is still known about what is actually killing the cabbage trees except that the disease is probably spread by a sap-sucking insect. However, the rate of loss is declining all the time and we are being left with those plants that are resistant to the disease, so keep planting these beautiful specimens and let's replace what we've lost.

The white butterfly caterpillar takes particular delight in the lush new unfurled leaves at the growing tips. As the buds open, the chewed leaves will become obvious, but the damage is purely aesthetic. If the plant is small, derris dust can be sprinkled throughout, ensuring that the new leaves are unfurled as far as possible. If the tree is too high to do this, a chemical systemic insecticide can be used.

Cordyline australis 'Purpurea'

If the cabbage tree is under stress, it can also get a form of rust that can be treated by spraying with copper oxychloride. After spraying, ensure that all other growing conditions are suitable — that it is not too wet or too dry, or hungry.

Cabbage trees naturally occur in quite swampy sites but if planting into one in warm humid areas, try and keep the ground cool by planting other species around it such as suitable *Carex* species or *Gunnera prorepens*. If *Cordyline australis* is stressed it can become susceptible to soil fungi such as *Phytophthora*, and keeping the ground cooler with shading like this limits the growth of such fungi.

CARE AND MAINTENANCE: Apart from caterpillars and rust, *Cordyline australis* is virtually maintenance free. If it is planted near an area that is to be mown, it is advisable to pick up any fallen leaves as they are too fibrous for the lawn mower to cut up and will clog the blade.

Cabbage trees propagate easily from seed.

LANDSCAPING SUGGESTIONS: The simple form of the cabbage tree allows it to blend with virtually any planting. It can be grown as a specimen or several as a small closely spaced grove in the middle of a lawn. To create a more natural look, flaxes and *Carex* species can be planted around the base with *Hebe macrocarpa* var. *macrocarpa*. Personally, I prefer to plant cabbage trees where the whole form of the tree is visible, but it can equally be planted among large broad-leaved shrubs, native or exotic, with the characteristic head protruding through the shrub layer.

If you would like this species to branch lower, you can plant a trunked specimen on an angle (which will encourage shoots to form on the exposed surface), remove the growing tip or you can try nicking the soft trunk with a knife or small axe, which can lead to branching from the damaged area. If using the latter methods, first ensure that the plant is growing vigorously so that it has the energy for shoot development and can heal itself, hence preventing fungal attack.

CULTIVARS:
• *C. australis* 'Albertii' has a cream variegation and grows to 4 m. It can branch from the base and is a good pot plant.
• *C. australis* 'Purpurea' is a purple-bronze form of *C. australis* but requires drier conditions.
• *C.* 'Green Goddess' is a cultivar with short

Cordyline banksii in full flower with its long weeping foliage

broad leaves and can branch from the base. It is very susceptible to root rot so requires very free-draining conditions and shelter if possible.
• *C. kaspar* is a wide-leaved form of cabbage tree that naturally occurs on the Three Kings Islands. It grows to around 3 m in height and can branch from the base. It requires dry conditions and is ideal as a pot plant.
• *C.* 'Purple Tower' is a strong purple colour and requires similar conditions to *C.* 'Green Goddess'.

SIMILAR SPECIES: *Cordyline banksii* (ti ngahere, forest cabbage tree) is smaller than ti-kouka at only 4 m. Its habit is different in that it naturally shoots from ground level but its flowering is just as spectacular. The old leaves fall freely from the branches leaving clear sculptural trunks.

A single ti ngahere can create the same effect as a cluster of *C. australis*, the multiple trunks creating the feeling of a magic forest. In a shaded dry environment, this species is outstanding and underutilised. The very long (1 m or more) broad leaves of ti ngahere, especially as a juvenile, are distinctive, as are the midribs, which can be bright red or even bright yellow. The broad-leaved nature of ti-ngahere makes it similar in appearance to *C. indivisa*, the striking, very broad-leaved cabbage tree of the central North Island. *Cordyline banksii* is much easier to grow in the north of the North Island, preferring cool, shaded free-draining sites. *Carex* species and low coprosmas such as *Coprosma* 'Black Cloud' could be planted around the base in the open, or ground ferns and shade-loving *Carex* species in lower light areas.

• 5–10 m tall
• Full sun to semi-shade
• Coastally hardy
• Wind hardy
• Tolerates very wet conditions
• Tolerates moderately dry conditions
• Frost hardy

Karaka is one of New Zealand's 'classic' trees, traditionally grown by Maori for its fruit. This forms in late summer/early autumn and is an important food source for some of the larger New Zealand birds, especially the native pigeon. The tree is relatively fast growing and upright in its habit and in a garden situation grows to a height of 5–10 m. In the forest it is a large canopy tree, sitting with its crown in the sunlight with species like taraire and puriri. The thick glossy green leaves are oval in shape and 10–15 cm long x 5–6 cm wide.

Karaka occurs naturally throughout the North Island and to Banks Peninsula in the South Island, more commonly in coastal bush although in the North Island it also occurs inland in lowland forests.

LIKES AND DISLIKES: In full sun karaka will form a tight-canopied tree, the habit becoming more open as the light levels decrease. Although it will tolerate

A young karaka tree

moderately dry conditions, this will slow the growth rate down considerably and it can take many months to re-establish itself. Stress can also be created by conditions that are too wet and through disease, although once the tree is well established this becomes less of a problem. Karaka needs good free-draining soil that has 'average' moisture levels. As long as the soil-moisture levels are maintained, exposure will not be a problem. It is tolerant of light frosts.

PESTS AND PROBLEMS: Black spot can be a problem in warmer, more humid areas, primarily on the soft new growth. This can be avoided by planting in an open spot, but if this is not possible and black spot is a problem, spray with a fungicide. Mites can also be a problem, causing the new leaves to be smaller and misshapen with the margins recurving, or rolling under. This should be dealt with as soon as it is evident, to prevent it spreading, by spraying with a systemic insecticide or miticide.

CARE AND MAINTENANCE: In general, karaka will require no pruning and can be just left to grow. When reshaped, it can take time to develop new buds and may not resprout as anticipated or may respond by coppicing (sprouting at the base of the plant). These new shoots can be pulled off by hand if they are not wanted. The new growth, wherever it forms, will be very vigorous and older wood may need to be removed to form a well-shaped tree with the new growth. Composting and mulching will help provide nutrients and retain soil moisture.

Karaka seed germinates very easily, although cuttings have to be taken for the variegated cultivars.

LANDSCAPING SUGGESTIONS:
Karaka's shape and size make it the perfect specimen tree, although the fruit can make quite a mess, so it is better as a garden specimen than a courtyard tree. Suitable

Clusters of karaka berries

underplantings include astelia, kawakawa, *Coprosma rhamnoides*, *Libertia* and *Carex*.

Karaka could also be used as hedging on its own or mixed with other plants like *Olearia*, akeake and ngaio; these three species are faster growing but ultimately the karaka will overtop them all, creating a height variance in the planting. Karaka is quite happy on the coast and can be kept bushy to the ground by pruning when young. A bushy karaka can look not unlike a *Griselinia lucida*, just a little more upright in its habit. In this form it could be planted with *Pachystegia*, Chatham Island forget-me-not, rengarenga and *Chionochloa*, with *Selliera radicans* and *Pimelea prostrata* as groundcovers. Karaka makes a good hardy indoor plant that will last a number of years.

CULTIVARS: *Corynocarpus* 'Albas Variegatus', 'Picturatus' and 'Variegatus' are variegated forms, all of which tend to be slower and smaller growing and a little more disease prone. They could be grown as pot plants.

- Tree 5–10 m tall
- Full sun to shade
- Dry tolerant as an adult
- Prefers a free-draining soil
- Wind tolerant
- Tolerates light frosts
- OK in coastal gardens

Ponga epitomises New Zealand to many; whether it was seen as such before it became our emblem is like trying to guess which came first, the tree fern or the emblem. The distinctive silver underside of the frond is where the common name comes from. Ponga ultimately reaches a height of around 5 m in a garden situation but is very slow to gain height. The trunk characteristically retains the silver bases of the fronds for a long time. Very young ponga fronds are green on both surfaces and as the plant ages the underside of the new fronds changes colour from the margins inwards. The upper green surface of all aged fronds is distinctively glossy. A relatively young tree fern just beginning to form its trunk will have fronds about 1 m long, but as the tree fern gains height the fronds grow longer, ultimately becoming 2–3 m long and about 1 m wide.

Ponga is found throughout New Zealand in lowland to montane forests.

LIKES AND DISLIKES: Ponga prefers a dry sheltered shaded environment but will tolerate open conditions, although the fronds will tend to become yellow-green and if it is windy, the margins of the leaves will become wind burnt. Ponga is tolerant of very dry conditions but if they are excessive, it may require some help establishing. Although tolerant of very light frosts, anything too severe will damage the fronds and possibly kill young plants.

PESTS AND PROBLEMS: It is a very easy species of tree fern to grow without any common pests or problems.

CARE AND MAINTENANCE: The old fronds can be cut off to keep the plant tidy. Compost and mulch will improve plant vigour, but remember to keep the crown of the fern clear while the tree fern is trunkless.

Fern propagation is difficult and requires patience and specialised conditions as the spore take time to develop and require just the right moisture levels while still avoiding fungal attack.

LANDSCAPING SUGGESTIONS: Ponga's preferred environment is best provided by established vegetation but can be created with a pergola or a roof overhang, remembering that the fronds will get to 2 m or more in length and that at some point it will very probably outgrow the structure. Suitable species to plant around a ponga are, of course, ground ferns like *Asplenium oblongifolium*, kiokio and native maidenhair ferns. Kawakawa, *Myrsine divaricata*, *Libertia* and native grasses will also add texture and colour to the planting.

SIMILAR SPECIES: *Cyathea medullaris* (mamaku or black mamaku) is even taller than ponga and has much larger fronds; it is the largest of all New Zealand's tree ferns. The space required to establish a mamaku has restricted its use in small inner-city gardens, even though it is often the preferred species of tree fern. It can be planted in full sun and is tolerant of some wind and moderate frosts. The down side is that it is prone to a fungus that attacks the crown, turning it

Ponga with new fronds

Silver underside of ponga fronds

to 'mush'. The warning sign is malformed fronds. If apparent, spray with a systemic fungicide immediately.

C. smithii (whe, soft tree fern) not only has the softest fronds but also requires the 'softest' growing conditions: moist, sheltered and shady. If conditions are too dry the fronds will wilt and the growing crown will die. This tree fern is very attractive, with many, almost lacy fronds out at one time.

> - Tree fern approx. 5 m high
> - Semi-shade to shade
> - Dry tolerant
> - Requires sheltered conditions

Mamaku

As a specimen, with its delicate often weeping habit, rimu is one of New Zealand's more spectacular species. Growing to a height of more than 40 m, it has an attractive pyramidal habit for the first 30–50 years, making it a large tree that can fit into a garden situation. Interestingly, there are separate male and female plants that as juveniles are indistinguishable. The needle-like foliage can vary from green to bronze in juvenile plants but tends always to be olive green as an adult. *FACT TIME: rimu flowers (and fruits) only once every five to seven years and is one of the main sources of food for the rare and endangered bird, the kakapo.* If you would like a female plant for its habit and/or its fruiting, you have two choices:

• Plant three juvenile plants; statistically there is a high probability that one of them

Young growth of rimu

will be a female. The Maori also have the belief that rimu should always be planted in groups of three and, what is more, they look good.

• Try and find a nursery producing female cutting-grown plants.

Rimu is found throughout New Zealand from quite swampy ground to dry regenerating hillsides.

LIKES AND DISLIKES: The habitats of rimu in the wild show its moderately wide moisture tolerance. It will tolerate quite wet situations if it has a cool root run — in the open in cooler climates or in the semi-shade where humidity levels are higher. Extremely dry situations are not ideal and should be avoided if possible but if you have no other choice, irrigation will be a necessity when the plant is young. Rimu will tolerate not only full sun but also quite shady sites, but the deeper the shade the slower the growth. Although rimu can tolerate a degree of exposure, it is better suited to more sheltered sites.

PESTS AND PROBLEMS: Rimu is not susceptible to any major pests or problems apart from very dry conditions, which can lead to foliage loss shown as browning off of the foliage.

CARE AND MAINTENANCE: Rimu is naturally a single-leader specimen and if you wish to maintain this habit, do not prune the top terminal branch. If you do, the tree will develop a number of main trunks and a bushier habit. Lower branches can be pruned without fear of losing the classic pyramidal habit. To help prevent the ground drying in the hot summer/autumn months, deep mulch can be spread around the base of the tree, ensuring the ground is moist beforehand and that no mulch is touching the trunk.

Seed is by far the easiest form of propagation, but this is not always readily available. Cuttings will root more readily, with fewer losses, if they are placed on a heat bed. Once the cuttings are established they will need to be trained into their more normal single-leader habit as they will initially continue to function as though they are branches. Once a shoot has attained dominance, all will be fine.

LANDSCAPING SUGGESTIONS: Rimu is restricted to gardens at least of a moderate size but it makes a wonderful specimen, either on its own or in a group. It can also be planted among other species in a border or a revegetation planting. Broad-leaved shrubs and trees contrast well with the needle-like foliage of rimu.

- 30 m tall
- Good specimen tree
- Full sun to shade
- Wet to semi-dry
- Moderately wind hardy

Wheki is not only the most common tree fern in the wild but also in cultivation. The logs of this species are used to build small retaining walls or placed upright and used as living fence palings. It is unusual among tree ferns in that it can sprout from the 'trunk', especially if the main crown is damaged, and what is more new 'trunks' can form from the underground root system a metre or more from the parent plant. These characteristics allow it to stay in existence after fire has ravaged an area, destroying most other species. It is the fastest growing, in terms of 'trunking', of all the tree fern species and has short fronds, hence requiring less space for establishment. The fronds are harsh to the touch and are dark green above and paler on the undersurface. Its relatively narrow 'trunk' ultimately reaches a height of 3–4 m in a garden situation.

Wheki occurs throughout New Zealand from sea level to 760 m.

Dicksonia squarrosa

LIKES AND DISLIKES: Wheki will tolerate full sun, a degree of wind exposure, frost, damp and dry conditions; where can it go wrong? If planted in full sun, it is advisable to plant around the base to help keep the root system cool.

PESTS AND PROBLEMS: In areas of high humidity wheki can lose its main crown through fungal damage, but this rarely kills the fern because it readily resprouts. It is advisable to spray the plant, and any others nearby, with a systemic fungicide to prevent infection of new growing shoots. This can be minimised by planting in an exposed position. Passion vine hoppers can be a problem on new fronds in warmer parts of New Zealand but they are very rarely lethal. Apart from that it is problem and pest free.

CARE AND MAINTENANCE: Wheki is a low-maintenance plant; the old fronds can be removed if so desired, and mulch and compost will improve its overall growth rate. When mulching remember to keep the crown of young tree fern clear as smothering will kill it. Propagation is as for *Cyathea dealbata*.

LANDSCAPING SUGGESTIONS: Wheki is very versatile. Logs can be planted in the ground, instantly creating a tree fern with a trunk. When trying this method it is advisable to plant in autumn when the ground is moist, and let the plant stabilise through winter and spring. If the site is moist the tree fern will require no further attention, but if it is dry it should be watered well through its first summer. This is best achieved by placing a dripper in the crown of the tree fern and letting the water permeate through the trunk to ground level. Another way of using logs is to lay them on the ground in among other vegetation that will help keep the trunk cool and prevent excessive drying out. The advantage is that the whole trunk is in contact with the ground, hence there is more area to form new roots. From these trunks new shoots will arise that will grow upright, forming new trunks. Similar species can be planted with wheki as for ponga.

Dicksonia fibrosa

SIMILAR SPECIES: *Dicksonia fibrosa* (wheki-ponga) is the slowest growing of the tree ferns and is often used by gardeners as a 'miniature tree fern' as it will take many years to even gain a few centimetres in height. The fronds are lighter in colour than wheki and the trunk is much thicker, covered in a dense layer of fibrous roots. It is similar to wheki in its environmental tolerances.

- Tree fern 3–4 m tall
- Full sun to shade
- Tolerant of dry conditions
- Tolerant of light winds

Akeake is very fast growing and forms a small often shrubby tree, particularly in exposed open sites. The pale green leaves, quite coarse to the touch, are not thick and are linear, approximately 4–10 cm long x 1–3 cm wide. As well as being a wonderful plant because of its hardiness, akeake has small bunches of creamy green flowers on the tips of branches and female plants form even more conspicuous seed capsules. These capsules, not unlike those of sycamore, are winged on both sides, forming a papery plate about 1.5 cm in diameter and a pale creamy green colour. Many people think that these are the flowers as they are a lot larger and hence more obvious than the flowers themselves. Akeake flowers in spring and seeds in summer.

This species occurs naturally throughout the North Island and in the South Island to Banks Peninsula on the east coast and to Greymouth on the west. Its habitat is coastal to lowland forest.

Bushy specimen of akeake

LIKES AND DISLIKES: The shadier the conditions, the more leggy akeake becomes, hence it is better grown in high light levels. In terms of exposure it can take it all, from exposed inland positions to salt-laden sea air. For soil moisture, akeake requires drier free-draining conditions and will not tolerate very wet soils.

PESTS AND PROBLEMS: The new leaves of akeake can become deformed by an insect, and this can be treated by spraying with insecticide. Thrips can also be a problem if the plant is stressed and can be combatted by spraying. Alleviating plant stress will also be effective, although the time frame will be longer. Apart from this, akeake is very easy to grow.

CARE AND MAINTENANCE: If akeake is growing too vigorously, it may require pruning to remove some of the lax soft growth and create a more upright plant. The soft new wood of akeake responds well to pruning but older secondary wood (see *Muehlenbeckia astonii* for an explanation of secondary wood) can be very slow and occasionally won't sprout at all. Mulch and/or compost will help keep the plant healthy and looking good but do keep it well away from the trunk of the tree.

The seed of akeake germinates very easily, but cuttings can be taken if that is the only material available.

LANDSCAPING SUGGESTIONS: Akeake can make an excellent hedge as it is not solid and just breaks the wind's flow. However, a mixed hedgerow creates more visual interest and structure. Akeake could be planted with *Olearia lineata*, ngaio, karo and the occasional ribbonwood to provide a slightly taller plant to break the line. These species all tolerate the same very exposed conditions, whether it be on a hilltop inland or on the coast. In a garden situation it can be planted with species like *Griselinia* or *Pseudopanax*, with which it will contrast. It could also be grown on its own as a specimen tree, pruning the lower branches off if necessary, leaving a clear-trunked tree. This could be used as a shade tree as akeake can become quite wide-spreading over time, and with the thin pale green foliage you would get lovely filtered light. If underplanting, species like *Corokia cotoneaster*, *Astelia*, *Polystichum vestitum*, maidenhairs and grasses are suitable. On the coast akeake could be planted with *Coprosma repens*, *Pachystegia*, *Muehlenbeckia astonii*, rengarenga and flaxes. This is a versatile species which is not used to its full potential. More adventurous florists use the foliage when the plant is in seed, as it does look quite spectacular and unusual.

Akeake seed capsules

Seed capsules of *Dodonaea viscosa* 'Purpurea'

CULTIVARS: *Dodonaea viscosa* 'Purpurea', purple akeake, is identical apart from its purple foliage and the purple hue to the flowers and seed capsules.

- Tree 4 m tall, up to 4 m wide
- Full sun to semi-shade
- Tolerates dry conditions
- Wind hardy
- Tolerates light frosts
- Coastally hardy

There is much confusion with the common name 'puka'. In the North Island the term is often used for *Meryta sinclairii*, while in the South Island it is used for *Griselinia lucida*. Here I am going to use puka as the common name for *Griselinia* and pukanui for *Meryta*. Next to pukanui, puka is probably the most 'tropical'-looking species in New Zealand. It has large thick glossy dark green leaves, up to 20 cm long x 10 cm wide. The bases of the leaves are unusual in that they join the petiole at different levels, higher on one side than the other. The plant is a very large multi-branched shrub that, if left untended in a rich free-draining soil, will send branches shooting off into the distance, metres in length. In the wild it is often epiphytic, perched on a tree, initially living on what moisture it can glean from the atmosphere and the hollow in which it is perched. As it establishes, it will send aerial roots down to the soil below. Epiphytic specimens tend to have larger leaves, as do

Puka foliage

specimens grown in the shade. The flowers are inconspicuous, as are the small dark purple fruit that develop afterwards on the female plants; these fruit are very attractive to birds.

Puka is found throughout New Zealand in lowland forest, although it tends to be more localised in its distribution in the South Island.

LIKES AND DISLIKES: The main intolerance of puka is soil moisture; it is very susceptible to *Phytophthora* hence it prefers a very dry free-draining soil. This is not surprising considering its epiphytic habit in the wild. It will tolerate full sun through to shade and wind exposure only limits its growth rate. It is slightly frost tender but the damage tends to affect only the fresh new shoots. It has been known to endure quite heavy frosts as far south as Christchurch.

PESTS AND PROBLEMS: The plant will show *Phytophthora* problems through a flattening of the leaf colour; the leaves will lose their gloss. If this happens, the ideal solution is to transplant the shrub as the site is obviously too wet. If, on digging up, all the roots are brown and rotten (thread-like), prune the plant back as severely as you think you can and transplant it into a dry situation; puka can come back from virtually nothing. If there are still good white roots, pruning need not be as severe. *HINT TIME: Before transplanting a severely affected plant check the base of the* plant where it joins the soil, and do a fine scratch on the bark just above soil level; if there is no green tissue, only black, the shrub is dead and can be thrown in the compost heap. In humid areas, fungus can affect the new shoots, turning them black, but this is very rarely lethal. It can be dealt with by spraying with fungicide. In general, planting in a dry position can prevent or alleviate most problems.

CARE AND MAINTENANCE: Puka requires little maintenance. If pruned regularly, it will be very bushy as it buds readily. If left unpruned, especially in warmer areas where the growth rate is more vigorous, puka will develop long shoots that will slowly form side branches up their length, resulting in an interesting shaped plant. If putting down compost or mulch, be very careful that none gets in contact with the trunk of the tree as puka is very vulnerable to collar rot.

Specimen of puka

Seed is the easiest method of propagation as cuttings are difficult to strike.

LANDSCAPING SUGGESTIONS: Puka is an underutilised species in New Zealand gardens. It bushes in the shade, is glossy and lush in appearance and will tolerate all situations apart from very severe frosts and wet soil. Some people consider it too wide spreading but this can be dealt with by judicious pruning from early on; there is no reason why it could not be trained into a single-leader tree, allowing it to spread at the desired height or it could be espaliered on a wall. To reiterate, puka is very prunable and can be shaped and reshaped! It is the perfect maintenance-free hedge if it has space to develop and can be left to grow at will. If there is not the space, it can be contained with pruning. The glossy green of the foliage is a perfect contrast to divaricating plants like weeping mapou, *Muehlenbeckia astonii* and grey-foliaged plants like *Astelia banksii* and *Brachyglottis* species. Even tall grasses like *Chionochloa* and *Carex secta* contrast well. The simple form and almost uniform colour make it a blank canvas to plant around — the picture is yours!

SIMILAR SPECIES: *Griselinia littoralis* (broadleaf or kapuka) has bright green leaves that are smaller than those of the puka. It has a more upright habit and is taller, growing to 6–7 m or more. It is equally prunable and as intolerant of wet conditions. It is more commonly known as a hedging species than puka. There are a number of variegated forms available but *Griselinia littoralis* 'Variegata' is probably the hardiest.

- Small tree 4–5 m tall
- 2–4 m wide, though very prunable
- Full sun to shade
- Dry tolerant
- Wet intolerant
- Wind hardy
- Tolerates moderate frosts
- Coastally hardy

The name New Zealand honeysuckle is erroneous as rewarewa is of the Proteaceae family, not the Caprifoliaceae family. The clue is in the rewarewa's wonderful red flowers, which form in late spring/early summer — the racemes can be up to 10 cm long and stand erect and upright on the tree, not unlike those of proteas. Rewarewa is a large tree, growing to 8 m in cultivation, with a very narrow upright pyramidal habit for many years of its life. The leaves are a lovely dark olive-green colour that contrasts with the rusty brown tomentum that clothes the new shoots, both leaves and branches. The serrated leaves of the juvenile plants are larger, up to 30 cm long x 4–5 cm wide, and softer than those of the adult, which are very coarse and much shorter at around 15 cm. The timber of rewarewa is beautifully speckled and the tree is very upright.

Rewarewa is found from North Cape in the North Island to the northern tip of the South Island, around Marlborough Sounds. It occurs from lowland to lower montane forests and in open scrubland.

Young rewarewa tree

LIKES AND DISLIKES: Damp situations should be avoided as rewarewa is very prone to root rot; if even a quite large tree becomes wet for a period, the main root structure can be destroyed and the plant will fall over. Conversely, rewarewa is very tolerant of dry conditions. It prefers full sun and if grown in shade will tend to be very straggly. It occurs naturally on recently disturbed land with manuka and kanuka, and will tolerate a degree of wind exposure, although if the wind is very strong and persistent, the edges of the leaves can become wind burnt.

Rewarewa flowers

PESTS AND PROBLEMS: The main disease problem is thrips, which shows as a significant paling of the leaves as the thrips feed on chlorophyll. Thrips rarely kills a plant and can be dealt with by spraying with a systemic insecticide. It generally only becomes a problem with a stressed plant, so ensure the plant is not too wet, too dry and/or very hungry. With spraying, plant vigour should return quite quickly. If left unsprayed, the plant will generally also recover although more slowly. Sometimes the plant will lose all its older damaged leaves, but the new growth that comes through will usually be clear of the problem, especially if the stress factor has been removed.

CARE AND MAINTENANCE: Like many large tree species, rewarewa responds relatively slowly to pruning, especially of older branches; the main shoot vigour is on the outer tips. Unless it is growing too quickly (see *Kunzea ericoides*), rewarewa should need little pruning. Mulching well annually should help prevent any thrips problem.

Seed is the main method of propagation; the thin papery seed germinate fairly quickly.

LANDSCAPING SUGGESTIONS: Although rewarewa is a moderately large tree its narrow habit allows it to fit into a smaller garden than other species that grow to a similar height. It could be planted as a specimen tree protruding through a mass planting of *Muehlenbeckia astonii* or red-flowering manuka, or as part of a large mixed planting with kanuka, *Pseudopanax* species, *Nestegis*, taraire and cabbage trees. It can also be planted along driveways or between buildings, where it will shoot up to the light and can be underplanted. Other suitable species for planting between buildings, if it is not too wet, are forest cabbage tree, tree ferns, *Pseudopanax laetus*, *Pseudowintera* and *Hebe diosmifolia*, with ground ferns and grasses.

- Tree 8 m tall
- Full sun to semi-shade
- Dry tolerant
- Wet intolerant
- Wind tolerant
- Frost tolerant

Kanuka and manuka are sometimes known by the combined name of tea tree, as the fresh leaves were once used to make tea (see *Leptospermum scoparium* for how to tell the difference between the two species). Kanuka is underutilised in domestic gardens, most often used when a large revegetation project is being undertaken. Although it grows to 15 m or more in the wild, kanuka tends only to grow to between 5 and 7 m in a garden situation. It is very fast growing and has an erect habit so will not encroach on other species, at least not until it gets close to its top height, when it will start to form a canopy. From an early age it will develop a clear trunk, whether in full sun or light shade. When the fine soft bright green leaves are crushed they release very fragrant volatile oils, sometimes used for their antiseptic and anti-fungal qualities. The small white flowers are only 3–7 mm in diameter but in summer can almost coat the tree, like a dusting of large snowflakes.

Young kanuka

Kanuka occurs throughout the North Island and in the South Island to the Clutha River on the east coast. It can be found in scrubland and forest margins from sea level to 900 m.

LIKES AND DISLIKES: Unlike manuka, kanuka does not like wet sites; it is, however, very tolerant of dry conditions. It prefers full sun but will tolerate light shade, tending to shoot up to find light; it tends to be very spindly until the leaves are in sunlight. Exposure is not a problem although it does slow the growth rate and create a tighter habit, as is the case with a majority of species.

PESTS AND PROBLEMS: Very occasionally kanuka will fall prey to manuka blight; some of the selected forms seem to be more susceptible (see *Leptospermum scoparium* for how to deal with this problem). Apart from this it is pest and problem free.

CARE AND MAINTENANCE: Kanuka rarely require pruning, although a young plant in rich soil can 'outgrow' itself, putting too much emphasis on primary upward growth and not enough on secondary thickening growth. If this does occur, prune it back a little and stake well. Kanuka responds relatively readily to pruning on young new growth but not at all on old growth, so prune carefully. Pruning the top heavily will not encourage growth lower down; most of the growth occurs in the upper parts of the plant. Composting and/ or mulching will en-courage growth but again the trunk of the tree should be left clear.

The seed is not always viable but if it is, it will begin germination within a month of sowing. Cuttings can also be taken; this will be necessary for the few cultivars that are beginning to be released.

Kanuka flowers

LANDSCAPING SUGGESTIONS: Kanuka are very difficult to transplant, so it is important to plant them in the right spot. Very small seedlings of 10 cm or so can be successfully transplanted, but as the size of the plant increases the likelihood of success decreases. Kanuka's rate of growth and hardiness make it an ideal hedging plant and, what is more, a flowering hedging plant. As the trunks begin to form, structure can be created with a second layer of planting. Suitable species for underplanting include *Hebe speciosa*, *Astelia* species, *Chionochloa flavicans* and other native grasses, and unpruned kaka beak, which can be allowed to trail in among the other plants. Kanuka could also be used in a large mixed planting with kowhai, *Griselinia*, rewarewa, lancewoods and a specimen or two of rata. A mature kanuka can also be a useful shade tree.

VARIETIES AND CULTIVARS: *Kunzea ericoides* var. *microflora* is a smaller-growing form from the central North Island volcanic areas. It grows to a height of about 50 cm. 'Cerise' is a selected form of this variety with a strong apricot to pink hue to the new growth, and older leaves that are much lighter in colour than normal kanuka. It can be covered in flowers in summer. It also reaches a height of about 50 cm and has a slightly spreading habit. Many production nurseries have their own selected forms of dwarf kanuka which are worth asking about.

- Tree 5–7 m tall
- Full sun to light shade
- Dry tolerant
- Wind tolerant
- Frost tolerant
- OK in coastal gardens

Pukanui is one of New Zealand's most tropical-looking plants, and a large plant in a garden looks quite striking. Plants can grow to at least 5 m tall x 2–3 m wide, but they can be contained. The thick glossy dark green leaves are up to 50 cm long x 20 cm plus wide. Initially a young plant will grow straight up, not unlike a cabbage tree, but when it flowers for the first time it uses its terminal bud and after that will branch from the main trunk. The flowers are inconspicuous. The black, ball-bearing-sized fruit form only on the female plants; as they begin to ripen, birds will move in.

Pukanui only occurs naturally on the Three Kings Islands and the Hen and Chickens.

LIKES AND DISLIKES: Pukanui is intolerant of frost, like many tropical plants, but it is completely wind tolerant. It is not affected by salt spray, and can tolerate living on coastal cliffs. Pukanui requires free-draining soil. If planted in a pocket of light in a generally shady site, it will shoot up until the leaves are in the sunlight before filling out; in full sun it will be shorter and stockier.

PESTS AND PROBLEMS: Pukanui is susceptible to *Phytophthora* in wet soil conditions, and above ground black spot can be a problem, especially in humid areas with little air movement. For both, spray with a systemic fungicide. Ideally, prune the plant back and move it to a drier location. Frost is a problem, and even if an area only gets one or two frosts a year, protection should be provided for at least the first two years of a plant's life, until the leaves thicken and it

Mature specimens of pukanui

gets above the frost layer. If a plant is frost damaged, the shoot will blacken and become very mushy. Prune the tip back until you find clean wood with no blackness in the centre. Spray the pruned plant with a systemic fungicide and protect it from frost for the rest of the season.

CARE AND MAINTENANCE: Pukanui is naturally very bushy, so it responds relatively quickly to pruning and will readily bud on the stem and main branches. Compost and/or mulch it regularly to keep it growing well.

The main method of propagation is seed. Cuttings can be taken but with limited success.

LANDSCAPING SUGGESTIONS: Pukanui is ideal for coastal situations, even in the South Island, if they are frost free. The lushness of the foliage makes it ideal as a backdrop for divaricating and small-leaved plants such as

Lush foliage of pukanui

Muehlenbeckia astonii, weeping mapou and *Coprosma virescens*. Possible contrast plants to put with pukanui are taraire, with its slightly bronzed leaves, *Hoheria* and ribbonwood with their soft leaves, totara with its needle-like leaves, mapou, *Hebe parviflora* and *Olearia* species. Pukanui can be trained to remain a single-leader plant at a specific height by rubbing off any new shoots as they form, leaving any that you want to develop. After a period the main stem will produce few, if any, new shoots. Pukanui also makes an ideal indoor plant.

CULTIVARS: *Meryta sinclairii* 'Moonlight' is a variegated form that is not readily available. The variegation is cream and yellow, with green only on the margins of the leaves. The lack of chlorophyll in the leaves means the plant is not very vigorous, hence cuttings do not take readily. This is a sought-after cultivar but it is expensive and disease prone. A variegated *Griselinia* cultivar may be a better choice.

- Tree 4–6 m tall, 2–3 m wide
- Full sun to light shade
- Dry tolerant
- Wet intolerant
- Wind hardy
- Frost intolerant
- OK in coastal gardens

Although pohutukawa only occurs naturally in the upper half of the North Island, it will tolerate warmer pockets of the South Island and will even grow happily in parts of Dunedin.

The classic form of the pohutukawa is open, wide sweeping and many trunked, but there are now selected forms available that are upright in their habit (see below). Pohutukawa have an unusual aerial root system; these fine roots can begin to form when the plant is but a few years old, and in some cases they hang from the main trunks and branches like red/grey spaghetti.

The lovely light-grey bark contrasts with the dark grey green of the adult foliage. The grey of the leaves is caused by a fine tomentum on the upper surface; the lower surface has a very dense tomentum and is completely grey. As a juvenile, the pohutukawa has plain green leaves with no tomentum on either surface. The flowers can vary from pink to quite deep red and all shades in between; there are even selected forms with yellow flowers. The flower buds can begin bursting in November, but more commonly December and January. Nectar-feeding birds love the flowers, and pigeons have been seen eating the whole thing!

Pohutukawa tree

Pohutukawa occurs throughout the upper half of the North Island to Poverty Bay on the east coast and Urenui on the west. It also occurs inland on shores of lakes in the Volcanic Plateau. It is found from sea level to 600 m.

LIKES AND DISLIKES: Adult-leaved pohutukawa are a lot hardier than juveniles, which are very frost tender and may become battered by strong coastal winds; some early protection may be required until adult leaves are formed. The other solution is to plant adult cutting-grown plants. Considering its natural habitat, it is not surprising that the pohutukawa prefers full sun and tolerates very dry conditions. It does not like wet feet.

PESTS AND PROBLEMS: In areas that have no pest management possums can still be a problem, eating the new growth. The other major pest is the psyllid, but while the lumps they cause on the juvenile leaves may look a little unsightly, they will not kill your plant. Psyllids do not feed on adult foliage so the effect disappears as the tree matures. If you cannot tolerate the 'look', the young tree can be sprayed with a systemic insecticide. The holes that can form on the leaves are caused by an insect. Spraying with a systemic insecticide will minimise these.

CARE AND MAINTENANCE: Pohutukawa require little care and maintenance. A juvenile plant grown in rich soil may initially form multiple primary branches; you can thin these to a selected few, or even to a single leader, if you like. As the tree ages it can be pruned to fit the space available, but choose your main branches carefully as it can take time to recover; once the new buds are formed, however, it can grow very rapidly. Composting and mulching will improve the plant's health and vigour.

Pohutukawa flowers

The fine dusty seed of pohutukawa tends to be consistently viable, although there are exceptions. Pohutukawa can be very slow growing for the first 2–3 years, so do not be surprised if the seedlings move very slowly; once the latter stages of juvenile foliage are reached they can grow very quickly. Cuttings can also be taken; this is necessary for the selected forms.

LANDSCAPING SUGGESTIONS: The pohutukawa has a very powerful root system and can find water where no other plant can; they have been known to lift houses off their piles and penetrate clay water pipes. Do not plant them near buildings or anywhere near any drainage system! They will eventually require a very large section or an arborist to keep them manageable. There are also selected forms available that supposedly only grow to 3–4 m, which are more suitable for a small section. The ground under large pohutukawa tends to be very dry so suitable species for underplanting could be rengarenga, *Chionochloa*, grasses and Marlborough rock daisy. In a garden where the soil is a little richer, hen-and-chicken fern, kiokio, *Libertia*, *Polystichum vestitum*, grasses and *Fuchsia procumbens* could be used. The size of the pohutukawa and the degree of shade it creates will influence what you plant under it.

CULTIVARS:
• *Metrosideros* 'Aurea' has sulphur yellow flowers.
• *Metrosideros* 'Maori Princess' has been selected for its upright habit and its limited aerial root system. It grows to around 7 m and has crimson flowers.
• *Metrosideros* 'Parnell' has been chosen for its shape, vigorous growth rate and because it is a profuse flowerer.
• *Metrosideros* 'Scarlet Pimpernel' has also been selected for its smaller, compact growing habit (3–4 m).
• *Metrosideros* 'Vibrance' has bright orange red flowers, like those of southern rata.

• Large tree 10 m or more in height
• 10 m or more in width, if allowed!
• Dry tolerant
• Wind hardy in adult foliage
• Tolerant of moderate frosts in adult foliage
• Wonderful in coastal gardens

Although it starts life as an epiphyte, northern rata will grow as readily as any other tree if planted in the ground. The young tree tends to be upright in its habit and any spreading forms that you see, with aerial roots, are probably pohutukawa hybrids; pure rata does not have aerial roots like the pohutukawa. Northern rata is not a fast-growing tree and can take a number of years to flower, but it is worth the wait. The deep red flowers contrast with the stiff dark green leaves, spearheaded in shape, with a characteristic small notch on the tip. The old leaves can be bright yellow through to red.

Northern rata occurs naturally throughout the North Island and to the Greymouth area in the South Island. It is found from sea level to 900 m.

Northern rata flowers

LIKES AND DISLIKES: Exposure is not a problem for northern rata but it is not fond of damp conditions and prefers high light levels.

PESTS AND PROBLEMS: See *Metrosideros excelsa*.

CARE AND MAINTENANCE: Northern rata will naturally form a clear trunk if left to grow on its own, but it can be pruned to shape. Be judicious when pruning as it does not bud readily. Compost and/or mulch, kept well away from the trunk, will improve plant growth, although it will still not be fast!

Propagation is by both seed and cuttings. When collecting seed make sure there are no pohutukawa around as they do hybridise readily. The woody cuttings can take some time to establish so a heat bed can be useful.

LANDSCAPING SUGGESTIONS: Northern rata makes a wonderful specimen tree but remember it is very slow growing and does better with higher light levels, so do not shade it out. If it is very small to start with, plant species like *Xeronema*, grasses and low-growing herbaceous plants around it, and as it grows include small shrubs like *Brachyglottis* and weeping mapou. The trunk of the tree is interesting so do not cover it completely. Northern rata can also be planted in a pot; as its root system is not too vigorous it will survive in a reasonable-sized container for many years. If planting northern rata in an old-established planting, try making an artificial epiphyte. Wrap the root ball in a thick wad of sphagnum moss and tie it all together, then find an old tree with a suitable, and accessible, nook to hold the rata, and tie the bundle into position. To help it get established over the first year or two you could tie an irrigation dripper into position, but do not over-water; the young plant has to learn to fend for itself. You may watch your own true rata develop, but don't hold your breath — you are doing it for a future generation!

SIMILAR SPECIES: *Metrosideros umbellata* is commonly known as southern rata. It is even slower growing than northern rata but has still more impressive flowers, although it tends to flower only sporadically. In the south, southern rata prefers damp cool soil, but in such conditions in the humid north it is very susceptible to *Phytophthora*. In such areas it prefers a free-draining soil but still a cool root run. It is much smaller than the northern rata, growing to only 4–5 m in cultivation, and in harsh conditions will form a dense shrub rather than a small tree.

Northern rata tree

- Tree 4–7 m in height
- Full sun to light shade
- Dry tolerant
- Wind tolerant
- Frost tolerant
- OK in coastal gardens

Juveniles of this species look quite unappealing; for the first few years they have a thin, stick-like look, with minimal side branches. As the tree develops its true beauty starts to become apparent. It has a classic tree shape, with a single clear trunk and rounded head. The dark green leaves are very willow-like in their form, though more leathery in texture, and they contrast well with the very pale, almost stark bark. The overall appearance of the tree is very soft and graceful. Oro-oro grows to around 5 m in a garden situation so is suitable for the smaller garden, unlike black or white maire, which can get significantly larger. The summer fruit borne on the female plants is bright red, 6–9 mm long.

Oro-oro occurs throughout the North Island and to around Nelson in the South. It is naturally found in lowland and lower montane forests, and commonly occurs in kauri forests.

LIKES AND DISLIKES: Oro-oro prefers drier, more free-draining conditions, but it is also tolerant of moist areas as long as the ground does not become waterlogged. It is tolerant of shade but will tend to stretch to find light, shooting up until it finds it then crowning out. Oro-oro is tolerant of windy conditions but they will reduce its growth rate and overall height.

PESTS AND PROBLEMS: Deformed new leaves can be dealt with by spraying with an insecticide, although the plant will tend to recover if stress is alleviated. Otherwise it is problem free. Compost and/or mulch well, ensuring the trunk of the tree is left clear.

CARE AND MAINTENANCE: It is best not to expose the plant to extremes of moisture conditions for the first few years, until the root system has established; after that it can be left to deal with its natural environment at its own pace. If a plant loses its terminal (apical) bud early on, it will become a multi-leader plant; these can look very sculptural, as the trunks will be clear lower down. If you prefer a single-leader plant, choose the strongest leader and prune the others off. Oro-oro does not bud readily after pruning, so be careful when undertaking this process.

Oro-oro seed can take up to two years to germinate as the seed is encapsulated in a hard nut. Cuttings can also be taken but they do not root readily; using bottom heat helps this.

LANDSCAPING SUGGESTIONS: This is an excellent small tree to plant in a garden if you want to attract birds, remembering that there are separate male and female plants. It can be planted as a specimen tree, or among other plants in a border or large planting. As the tree forms a clear trunk, the base can be planted with lower-growing plants such as kawakawa, *Muehlenbeckia astonii*, and a variety of ground ferns. To make the most of the pale trunk, ensure that you do not plant any taller-growing species in your line of sight. If planting oro-oro in a group planting, try mixing it with *Meryta sinclairii*, lancewood, taraire, kowhai and even tree ferns to add another texture.

- 5 m tall, 3 m wide
- Full sun to shade
- Tolerant of dry conditions
- Tolerant of windy conditions
- Frost tolerant

Silver beech forms a magnificent specimen tree, with tiers of branches and layers of leaves lying flat, facing upwards towards the sunlight. It is relatively slow growing, with a classic form. In cultivation it can attain a height of around 10 m. The small dark green foliage is approximately 1 cm x 1 cm and is finely toothed, and contrasts with the silvery coloured bark of the older wood. A mature tree can have a large, spreading canopy if there is room, but it will also fit into the available space.

Silver beech occurs naturally from the Thames area south through the rest of New Zealand. It is found from sea level to subalpine scrub, where it often forms but a small bush.

LIKES AND DISLIKES: As with most species of New Zealand beech, silver beech requires moderately high light levels to grow. In beech

Young silver beech

forest small seedlings of only 30 cm may be 20 years old; once a gap forms in the canopy they will shoot up to fill the space. In warmer areas beech requires a cool root run, which can be provided by other species which protect the soil from the direct heat of the sun. An open-canopied tree like kowhai can provide excellent protection while still allowing light through; as the beech grows the kowhai can be pruned to allow the beech to continue upward where it will eventually form a canopy over the kowhai. In humid areas beech is susceptible to root rot so it should be planted in free-draining soil. Further south it can tolerate a wide range of soil conditions and is quite tolerant of wind exposure.

PESTS AND PROBLEMS:
There are no major pests or problems with beech trees.

CARE AND MAINTENANCE:
Beeches require little attention after planting. Some pruning may be necessary to create the shape you require, but silver beech is quite tolerant if you prune the young wood. The older the wood the less likely the plant is to resprout. Mulch and/or compost will improve the plant's growth and health, but do not put it close to the trunk of the tree.

Silver beech foliage

Seed is the normal method of propagation but it should be sown straight away as it does not remain viable for very long.

LANDSCAPING SUGGESTIONS: Planted in the open, in a park-like setting, silver beech can look magnificent, but it can be pruned to keep its height down if you have limited room. If doing the latter, don't let the tree get too tall before you start to shape it, and choose your branches carefully to create a miniature version of a large tree. Because it does not grow quickly it will only need pruning once a year, or even less in some areas. It can also be used as an emergent tree in a mixed planting; plant it with *Hoheria*, *Pseudopanax*, maire, kowhai and nikau.

SIMILAR SPECIES: *Nothofagus fusca* (red beech) is one of the fastest growing of the native beeches. The leaves are larger than those of silver beech and more coarsely toothed. The reddish growth of young plants is strongest in the winter. In spring, when the new growth forms, the plant will often drop most of the previous year's leaves. It requires similar growing conditions to silver beech.

Nothofagus solandri (black beech), which has small oval leaves, is sometimes considered to be less attractive than red or silver beech, but it still creates an impressive specimen tree. It is wind hardy and slightly more tolerant of extremes of conditions. *Nothofagus solandri* var. *cliffortioides* (mountain beech) is smaller growing and again very hardy. It is suitable for smaller gardens.

> • Tree 8–10 m tall
> • Full sun to semi-shade
> • Requires a cool root run in warmer areas
> • Wind tolerant
> • Frost hardy

This is one of New Zealand's fastest-growing trees. It is also one of our largest-growing deciduous trees, although it is only semi-deciduous in the far north. A fully grown tree will be 6–8 m tall. The juvenile plant is very attractive with its almost divaricating habit, smaller leaves than the adult plant, and fine weeping branches that interweave among one another. This form continues until the tree is about 2 m tall, when it starts to slowly change to its adult habit. The adult tree has its own beauty. It can be a single- or multi-trunked tree, depending on whether the main growing tip has been damaged or not. It is one of the few New Zealand natives that can readily be coppiced; if the tree is cut near the base, a number of new stems will quickly develop, producing a tree with many trunks, almost shrub-like in its form. The leaves of the adult tree are very soft and shaped like spear-heads, with irregularly serrated margins. It

Juvenile ribbonwood foliage

is not uncommon for the adult tree to carry some juvenile foliage. The trunks tend to lose their lower branches and the upper branches slowly spread to form a moderately open canopy. The very pale green flowers are only 3–4 mm in size, but they group together to form large hanging 'bouquets' 25 cm or more long. In summer a tree can be festooned with these, and the effect continues for many months as the flowers dry and the seed capsules form. The flowers are normally unisexual but can be both sexes.

Ribbonwood occurs in localised pockets throughout New Zealand, with the exception of the tip of the North Island. Its habitat tends to be lowland forest.

LIKES AND DISLIKES: Ribbonwood is tolerant of dry soils through to wet, and of poor soils. In full sun its habit tends to be tighter than in shade, but it is tolerant of light shade. Ribbonwood is not frost tender, and the divaricating habit of the juvenile plant provides protection from strong winds.

PESTS AND PROBLEMS: Ribbonwood is susceptible to a number of diseases. If the leaves are wilting and slowly dying back, remove all the damaged foliage back to clean growth and spray with an insecticide. Cut out any galls where possible. If the leaves have distorted areas with yellow or brown spots, or are grey underneath, spray with a fungicide. Ribbonwood is also susceptible to borer. The infected wood can be cut out or insecticide injected into the holes.

CARE AND MAINTENANCE:
Prune as desired. The lower branches on a mature tree may persist in their juvenile form, but they can easily be pruned off. Mulch and com-post will both improve plant growth, but make sure the trunk is left clear.

Seed is the most common form of propagation but cuttings can be taken, especially if you want a sexed plant.

LANDSCAPING SUGGESTIONS:
Ribbonwood is ideal in a coastal situation, and it can be an excellent shade tree for the garden, for both plants and people. Underplant with species like *Astelia banksii*, *Chionochloa flavicans*, native irises, *Polystichum vestitum* and *Muehlenbeckia axillaris*. In a damp site *Mazus radicans*, *Asplenium bulbiferum*, kiokio and *Carex secta* could be planted. Ribbonwood can also be used as a specimen tree in a large planting, with only its crown poking through; plant it with mapou, manuka cultivars, *Olearia lineata* and *Pseudopanax* species. Being fast growing, it is an ideal hedging species; once it has moved into its adult form it can be underplanted to create a structured hedge line.

SIMILAR SPECIES: *Hoheria populnea* (houhere or lacebark) can look very similar to ribbonwood as an adult plant and is equally fast growing. In cultivation it tends to be more disease prone than either ribbonwood or *Hoheria sexstylosa*.

Hoheria sexstylosa is less well known. As an adult tree it is also very similar to ribbonwood and at least as fast growing. It tends to be less disease prone than the other *Hoheria* species. It does not have the divaricating juvenile habit of ribbonwood but juvenile plants do have smaller, irregularly shaped leaves that enlarge on maturation.

Divaricating juvenile ribbonwood

Adult ribbonwood foliage

- Tree 6–8 m tall
- Full sun to semi-shade
- Dry tolerant
- Wet tolerant
- Wind hardy
- Frost tolerant
- OK in coastal gardens

Although a large tree, totara is more versatile than many people think. In the garden it tends to grow to a height of 5–10 m, not the 30 m or so that it can reach in the forest. The juvenile totara can look very spindly, with its fine needle-like leaves and sparse, thin, almost weeping branches, but as the tree matures the pale olive-green leaves become shorter and less needle-like and the branches stouter and stronger; slowly the form of the mature tree starts to show through. As with many of New Zealand's podocarps, such as rimu and kahikatea, totara has a pyramidal 'adolescent' habit. As the tree continues to mature, the lower branches fall by the wayside and a wonderful straight clear trunk begins to emerge. Very old trees that have grown in the open for hundreds of years can start to form a magnificent spreading habit that is seen at its best if the old, dead or unproductive branches are removed. If totara is cutting grown from an

Young totara tree

adult plant it will tend to have a bushy habit, although it can be trained into a single- or multi-leader plant with judicious pruning. The bark of totara is a lovely red-brown colour and peels off in long strips on mature trees. Totara has separate male and female plants; the small bright red receptacles that bear the seed are only found on the female plants.

Totara is found throughout New Zealand from lowland to subalpine forests. It is commonly a ridge species, preferring the often drier conditions there.

LIKES AND DISLIKES: Although totara is tolerant of very dry conditions it is best to maintain adequate moisture levels for the first few years of establishment, otherwise you can lose any new growth and the plant becomes stressed. Conversely, in very wet, warm conditions totara can be susceptible to root rot, which can be lethal. Totara will tolerate quite shady conditions but will tend to be more elongated in its habit; full sun or semi-shade is better.

PESTS AND PROBLEMS: Totara is generally pest and problem free.

CARE AND MAINTENANCE: Young totara grow into stockier, hardier plants if they are initially planted in poor soils. If the soil is too rich juvenile, totara will put too much energy into new shoot development and become very 'whippy' in their habit. Once the plant starts to move out of its juvenile habit it will be less affected by high nutrient levels. If you want a single-leader specimen, ensure that the main growing tip is not damaged; if it is, a multi-leader plant will develop. To overcome this you can choose one of the new shoots that develop at the top and train it into a main leader. Conversely, if you want a bushy tree and it is not cutting grown, remove the tip.

Seeds are the main form of propagation, as they are easy to germinate. Totara do not seed every year, but when they do they are formed in abundance. Cuttings are also taken, but being woody they take some time to form roots; they benefit from bottom heat.

Golden totara

LANDSCAPING SUGGESTIONS: Totara is wonderful as a specimen tree and can be maintained to suit a smaller garden. Its natural habit also makes it an excellent shade tree. When planting under an established totara, remember that conditions there will be very dry; suitable species include *Asplenium oblongifolium*, *Hebe diosmifolia*, *Libertia* and *Astelia banksii*. Cutting-grown totara readily forms a dense tree that is easily pruned and consequently can be used as a hedging species. A well-tended totara hedge can look rather like a macrocarpa hedge.

CULTIVARS: *Podocarpus totara* 'Aurea' (golden totara) is cutting grown so will have a bushy habit unless trained otherwise by pruning. It is ideal for hedges.

- 5–10 m in a garden situation
- Full sun to shade
- Wind tolerant
- Dry tolerant
- Frost hardy
- OK coastally

The juvenile lancewood looks quite sculptural, as it grows very quickly straight upward, though occasionally it has an interesting kink. There is usually only one stem; if there is more than one, it is normally because the main growing tip has been damaged. When this occurs the tree can be even more sculptural — as the tree ages its appearance is enhanced by the narrow, rope-like look of the trunks. The leaves of the juvenile plant are very long and thin — 50 cm or more long x 1–2 cm wide. These saw-toothed leaves are very thick and hang individually from the main stem. Inter-estingly, if a leaf is knocked or falls off, it is not replaced; all the new leaves are formed from the apical bud — so be careful when dealing with young lancewoods. As the tree matures the leaves change in shape and colour. Juvenile leaves can vary from green

Juvenile lancewood

through to yellow green; the coarse midrib is different again, varying from a green yellow right through to red and all shades in between. The adult leaves are much shorter and broader, and a glossy dark green colour. The serrations on the leaves are also a lot less pronounced. The overall appearance of an adult tree is of a branchless trunk and a tight glossy green head — very different from the juvenile plant but equally pleasing.

Lancewood is found throughout New Zealand from sea level to 760 m. It occurs naturally in lowland and lower montane forests and scrublands.

LIKES AND DISLIKES: The lancewood dislikes excessive moisture, so a dry or free-draining soil is ideal. It will tolerate full sun to quite shady conditions, although in shade it will tend to be very stretched and not take on the adult form until it reaches the light. The thick leaves help prevent wind damage so exposure is not a problem.

PESTS AND PROBLEMS: Humidity is not a problem with lancewood but in heavy wet soils it can be very susceptible to *Phytophthora*. Then there are rabbits — rabbits love young lancewood and will happily go through your planting and take the tips out of every one. If there are rabbits in the area, fence the plants until they are out of reach.

CARE AND MAINTENANCE: Lancewood is not a tree you can prune and it has no real pest or disease problems; a species to plant and watch grow!

Seed is the normal method of propagation.

LANDSCAPING SUGGESTIONS: Lancewood looks good with virtually any other plant. Because the trunk of the tree is so stunning, the planting in front of it should ideally be low enough to show it off. A glossy-leaved plant in the background, like puka or pukanui, will also accentuate the trunk and the juvenile form of lancewood. A contrasting wall will do the same thing. To create a multi-stemmed specimen, be brave and cut off the main growing tip. The young plant will tend to form a number of new buds from the cut face, so choose your height and cut! A wonderful grove of multiple-stemmed lancewoods can be created, with short native grasses making a soft floor underneath. For variation add the odd divaricating plant, like weeping mapou or *Muehlenbeckia astonii* or, for a slightly different look, clumps of astelias with the odd *Asplenium oblongifolium*. If in doubt about what to do with your lancewood, put it in a planter, ensuring it has good drainage and no saucer underneath to cause waterlogging.

SIMILAR SPECIES: *Pseudopanax ferox* (toothed lancewood) has juvenile leaves that are shorter and much thicker than those of *P. crassifolius*, and have very defined teeth, almost like a shark. They are grey black and stick out more vertically from the plant. Toothed lancewood is even more intolerant of wet soil, so plant in very free-draining soil. It is very, very, very slow growing but has an even more beautiful trunk than the ordinary lancewood.

- Tree 5–6 m tall
- Full sun to shade
- Dry hardy
- Wet intolerant
- Wind hardy
- Frost hardy
- OK in coastal gardens

Adult lancewood

Juvenile (left) and adult *Pseudopanax ferox*

Nikau is New Zealand's only palm. It is very slow growing, even slower than a kentia palm. The long fronds can reach 2 m in length before the plant even begins to form a trunk, which can take 15 years or more. As the plant matures the bulbous sheath from which the fronds emerge becomes more obvious. The trunk of the nikau is scarred with rings from old fallen leaves and no, these rings do not give a visual record of how old the plant is. In some years it may form two or three fronds and in others none at all. In shaded bush settings nikau can reach 10 m or more in height, but in light shade it tends to be much shorter. It can take 30 years for nikau to start flowering and hence fruiting; it has large panicles of small pinkish purple flowers and red fruit, which hang from just below the base of the leaves. The fruit take a year to develop. There is some genetic diversity of nikau throughout New Zealand and its offshore islands. The nikau of Great Barrier and Little Barrier Islands tend to have larger fronds and be taller; the

Mature nikau with a cluster of fruit

West Auckland nikau is considered a 'ratty' example of the species, while the West Coast of the South Island has a favoured form. Nikau from the Chatham Islands and the Kermadecs have broader fronds and a denser habit, and many landscapers believe they are more tolerant to exposed situations.

Nikau occurs throughout the North Island, and to Banks Peninsula on the east coast of the South Island and Greymouth on the west. It tends to reside in shaded river valleys of lowland forests.

LIKES AND DISLIKES: Nikau does not like being transplanted, so choose its position with care. Ideally it should be spacious, shady and moist, and have rich soil. Nikau can be planted in full sun but the fronds will tend to be more upright; if it is also exposed to wind, the tips of the fronds may burn off. If planting in full sun, ensure the roots are shaded, either by rocks or other low-growing plants, as it requires a cool root run. Nikau will tolerate light frosts only.

PESTS AND PROBLEMS: Nikau has no real pests or problems as long as it has a cool root run.

CARE AND MAINTENANCE: Ensure your nikau is well mulched and/or composted every year. The mulch will help keep soil moisture levels up, improve soil structure and provide nutrients. Although nikau prefers moist soil it does not like water-logged soil.

Seed is the only means of propagation, and it can take two years or more to germinate. To speed up the process try using seed in which the fruit is only just starting to change to a pink colour.

LANDSCAPING SUGGESTIONS: In quite shady situations the fronds of nikau will open out to form a large bowl-like structure, so it will eventually take up a lot of room until it starts to trunk. Since this time frame is relatively long, plant other shade-loving species around the young nikau, such as ferns, *Astelia banksii* and *Carex dissita*. In semi-shade or sun the fronds will tend to be more upright and other planting will not be so affected by them. Like most species of palm, nikau is an excellent pot plant.

- Up to 10 m in height
- Shade to semi-shade
- Rich, free-draining soil
- Sheltered site
- Tolerant of light frosts

Nikau fruit

Nikau fronds

The magnificent bright yellow flowers of the kowhai are a welcome sign of spring to both humans and many species of native bird. Each flower is about 4 cm long, and they form in clusters of 4–10. In many parts of New Zealand the kowhai is deciduous, losing its leaves through the winter months. When this is the situation the flowers are even more prominent, as they often form before the new spring leaves. *Sophora microphylla* has a divaricating juvenile habit. The fine young branches are yellow and have a wonderful zigzagging habit, the overall form looking like a large Japanese bonsai. As the tree matures the branches stretch and thicken. *S. microphylla* can take up to 10 years to flower. The delicate leaves of *S. microphylla* can be up to 15 cm long and are made up of a number of very small leaflets. Unfortunately, *Sophora tetraptera* and *S. microphylla* readily hybridise so it can be difficult to purchase a pure species, especially of *S. tetraptera*.

Sophora microphylla* occurs throughout New Zealand in forest margins, beside rivers, coastally and in other generally open areas.

Kowhai in full flower

LIKES AND DISLIKES: There is a common misconception that kowhai will tolerate damp or wet conditions. In fact, the kowhai likes a rich free-draining soil, and if the soil does become waterlogged, it will eventually die, especially in warm humid areas. Although it can occur naturally on riverbanks, these tend to be free draining in their soil structure, or very stony. Kowhai prefers a sunny site although it will tolerate some shade. It will also tolerate coastal and very cold situations, but the growth rate will be slower.

PESTS AND PROBLEMS: The kowhai moth caterpillar can defoliate a plant very quickly, especially if the plant is small or if it is infested. The caterpillar tends to go for the lush new shoots first but it will move on to the older leaves once these are gone. An insecticide will need to be applied to deal with the problem. If the plant is small, derris dust can be sprinkled over it, or the caterpillars can be plucked off by hand! The latter requires good eyesight but is very satisfying. Generally the plant will slowly recover from even complete defoliation, so do not panic if this happens. The other major pest is borer, which will show as small holes in the trunk or branches and/or fine wood dust around the holes or on the ground at the base of the plant. Borer greatly affects the growth of the plant and will eventually lead to its demise. Cut out infected wood if possible; if not, inject insecticide.

If your kowhai is planted in a damp spot, you will have to move it or lose it! If this is the only spot in the garden of a suitable size, try lifting the root ball to ground level and mounding compost and topsoil around it.

CARE AND MAINTENANCE: Apart from keeping a vigilant eye out for signs of the pests described above (remembering that kowhai can be deciduous) these plants are virtually maintenance free. But do remember to keep compost and mulch well away from the trunk of the tree.

LANDSCAPING SUGGESTIONS: The natural upright but open habit of kowhai makes it an ideal light shade tree. It is also moderately fast growing. If underplanting in exposed sites, lush species such as *Myosotidium hortensia* and *Heliohebe hulkeana* could be planted with *Pachystegia insignis*. Another option is to underplant entirely with *Chionochloa flavicans* or some other native tussock grass. Its delicate weeping foliage and striking spring flowers also mean that kowhai can add form and colour to any mixed tree and/or shrub planting.

SIMILAR SPECIES: *Sophora tetraptera* has larger leaves and flowers and can be taller. It does not have a divaricating juvenile habit and can begin flowering earlier, at 5–7 years.

Sophora microphylla var. *fulvida* occurs naturally only on the west coast of the Auckland area. It tends to be more erect in its habit and smaller in stature, at only 3–4 m. The new growth also has a soft yellow-brown tomentum.

Sophora 'Dragons Gold' is a low-growing spreading form that attains a height of only 1.5–2 m. It is unusual in that it is evergreen throughout New Zealand and it is a winter flowerer, providing food for nectar-feeding birds at a time when there is little around. The flowers are a little larger than those of *S. microphylla* but form singly, not in clusters.

Sophora prostrata is a dwarf kowhai (2 m) with a divaricating habit. The flowers are a yellow orange and are borne singly and sporadically.

- 3–7 m tall, 3–4 m wide
- Dry tolerant
- Wet intolerant in humid areas
- Full sun to semi-shade
- Frost hardy
- Coastally hardy

Puriri is another very large, often spreading tree. It is not unlike pohutukawa in its form, especially if grown in the open, where an old plant can have a spread of many metres. The branches can become so large and heavy that they slowly fall to ground level, where they may even develop new roots. In the forest puriri can form a tree with a massive trunk, sometimes over 1.5 m in diameter, which extends upwards to the canopy where the tree opens, filling the space available to it. These trees are many hundreds of years old. While puriri is not fast growing, neither is it slow — it is one of those species with an 'average' rate of growth. The leaves are made up of a number of serrated-edged leaflets that are joined together like the fingers on a hand. They are bright green through to dark green, depending on the light levels; the more light there is, the lighter the colour. A mature puriri tree flowers, and hence fruits, sporadically through the year and is rarely devoid of fruit; it is therefore wonderful for attracting birds. The 2–3 cm long, tubular flowers are bright pink and occur in small groups. Fruit, which look like pink-red marbles suspended in the tree, follow the flowers. These are about 2 cm in diameter.

Puriri only occurs in the North Island, from the Mahia Peninsula and Taranaki northwards. It grows naturally from the coast through to lowland forests.

LIKES AND DISLIKES: Puriri prefers a moist free-draining soil, and in these conditions will have a moderate rate of growth. It is tolerant of dry conditions but the growth rate will be greatly reduced. If it becomes so stressed that it ceases to grow, it can take a year or more to

Mature puriri trees

recover. Hence, it is advisable to provide a young plant with adequate moisture. Puriri is intolerant of wet conditions, however, as it is prone to root rot. It will tolerate full sun through to shade and a moderate amount of exposure, although some shelter early on will be beneficial.

Puriri foliage and flowers

PESTS AND PROBLEMS: The main pest problem is puriri moth, the larvae of which burrow into branches of the tree, and even that is uncommon. The holes that are formed can be injected with kerosene and plugged, or infected growth removed.

CARE AND MAINTENANCE: Puriri is very easy to look after, especially if it has the right conditions. Prune if necessary, otherwise leave it to grow. Mulch and/or compost will improve soil fertility and improve soil moisture levels and hence improve the growth rate.

Seed is the normal means of propagation, and occurs within the woody covering under the fleshy fruit.

LANDSCAPING SUGGESTIONS: This is naturally a large tree which looks at its best when given the freedom to grow. It provides a lovely backdrop, and anything can be planted with it. It can also be pruned to fit the space available; to create the best shape, begin to prune it before the plant is too big. It can be kept as a bush if there is enough light, or it can be pruned to create a small single- or multi-leader canopy tree. Although puriri is considered a coastal tree, it will grow more vigorously if provided with a little shelter; either plant it in a leeward gully or slight hollow, or shelter it with hardier species like pohutukawa, ngaio, akeake or *Olearia lineata*. It could be underplanted with *Myrsine divaricata*, rengarenga, *Machaerina* and ground ferns like *Polystichum* and *Asplenium*.

- Large tree 10 m+
- Width as you wish!
- Dry free-draining soil
- Wet intolerant
- Wind tolerant
- Tolerant of very light frosts only
- OK in coastal gardens

Makamaka could be termed a small tree or a large shrub. In a sunny garden situation it will grow to a height of 3–4 m, with a lovely spreading, sometimes open habit, while in the shade it can grow to 6 m plus and be more upright, even single leader, in its form. Both forms are entirely natural and require no pruning to maintain them. The soft leaves are made up of a number of toothed leaflets that attach to the main midrib in pairs. Some have a delightful pinky-red hue to the underside of the leaves and new branches, most noticeable when standing under a mature tree and looking up. Check the underside of the leaves when you purchase the plant, as not all makamaka have this. The very small cream flowers that form in spring occur in large panicles and can look quite striking hanging from the plant like bundles of cotton wool. Although makamaka does not have fruit per se, it has wonderful pinkish red seed capsules, similar in colour to the underside of the leaves,

Makamaka flowers and foliage

which hang in large clusters through late spring and early summer. If you have the right conditions, it is a lovely small tree for a city garden.

Makamaka occurs naturally from Kaitaia to Whangarei, on forest margins and along streambanks.

LIKES AND DISLIKES: Makamaka has strong likes and dislikes! It is quite frost tender, it requires protection from high winds, and it is drought intolerant. If the garden is at all dry, makamaka will be one of the first species to tell you — it wilts! If it is dry for any length of time, it will often die. It is advisable only to plant makamaka if you have a frost-free site that is moist all year round, not just in winter! However, it will tolerate full sun through to reasonably shady sites.

PESTS AND PROBLEMS: There are no major pests or other problems to worry about.

CARE AND MAINTENANCE: Make sure the plant does not dry out, mulch it well, and prune it to shape if you wish. Makamaka does not bud readily after pruning, so cut judiciously. If it does dry out and wilt, prune it back quite hard to reduce stress, and water well for at least 3–4 weeks.

Do not drown the plant though, as this can create its own problems in a plant that is already under stress. *TIP TIME: One stress at a time is a good basic rule! Secondary infections can easily develop, just as humans are prone to getting pneumonia when they are very ill!*

Seed is the normal method of propagation although cuttings can be taken. It is a woody species, so cuttings may take some time to develop roots.

LANDSCAPING SUGGESTIONS: Only plant makamaka if you have the right conditions for it. You can irrigate, but remember irrigation can fail! In the right conditions makamaka can be wonderful planted on its own as a small specimen tree, especially in full sun or semi-shade. In full sun it can be bushy to ground level; if you don't like this look, prune the

Mature makamaka

lower branches off and underplant with *Asplenium bulbiferum*, *Blechnum pennamarina*, *Mazus radicans* and suitable grasses. As makamaka can tolerate a high water table it is ideal for planting around a dam, where it can be planted with *Carex secta* and *Phormium tenax*, with *Gunnera prorepens* as a groundcover.

- Large shrub 3–6 m tall
- Full sun to shade
- Dry intolerant
- Wet tolerant
- Prefers shelter
- Frost tender

Aristotelia serrata • MAKOMAKO, WINEBERRY

In the wild, makomako is very common on damp, disturbed forest margins. It has a very fast growth rate, especially in rich soil, which makes it ideal where cover is required quickly or in a new garden. Makomako will grow to a height of 3–4 m in a garden situation but it responds very quickly to even quite hard pruning, so it can be restricted to whatever height or shape you want. The soft, serrated leaves are reasonably large and shaped rather like a spade on a playing card. The colour can vary from quite dark green to a mottled olive green and bronze; the undersides of the leaves can have a purplish hue. *FACT TIME: Maori use the leaves for relieving back problems. The leaves are placed in a porous bag and steeped in a hot bath, into which you then climb.* Makomako has separate male and female plants and you will require both sexes even to get fruit on the female plant. *FACT TIME AGAIN: In many species with separate male and female plants, the female will still produce fruit but not viable seed.* The dark red berries are very attractive to birds. The delicate, rosy coloured flowers are borne on short panicles in early spring. As the flowers age they darken in colour, creating a wonderfully colourful effect. Makomako is only semi-deciduous in warmer areas, and the flowers are more prominent in colder climates, where they form on bare stems with the spring leaf growth just beginning to pop.

Makomako is found throughout New Zealand, especially on disturbed sites, from lowland forest to 1060 m.

LIKES AND DISLIKES: In general makomako is very hardy. It will tolerate full sun to moderate shade, where it will become more tree-like in its form. Damp conditions are not a problem, but

Makomako foliage

it will wilt, although not necessarily die, in excessively dry conditions. In exposed situations the leaves thicken and the plant becomes more compact.

PESTS AND PROBLEMS: Makomako can get powdery mildew, which will show as a fine white powder on the new shoots and the leaves will become distorted. If this happens, spray with fungicide. In warmer areas, passion vine hopper can be a problem. A systemic insecticide or regular sprayings with a contact insecticide will control the infestation for a while. Passion vine hoppers are rarely lethal, but they will slow the growth of the plant.

CARE AND MAINTENANCE: If the plant is growing very vigorously it may require pruning to keep the height down or to shape it. As always, a good layer of mulch will help retain plant vigour; remember to avoid contact with the trunk of the tree.

Mature makomako

Propagation can be by seed or cuttings. To ensure a specific sex, cuttings will need to be taken from plants identified at flowering.

LANDSCAPING SUGGESTIONS: To provide instant structure in a new garden, plant makomako in among slower-growing shrubs and trees, keeping it pruned so it does not overshadow the other plants. Later it could be dug out and transplanted. Makomako can also be planted as a specimen shrub, perhaps with an underplanting of ground ferns, *Libertia* species and native grasses. It can also be used as an 'instant' hedge, which will be easy to maintain and hardy. If you pick your plant, the colour of the foliage can add an unusual bronze hue to the garden. Makomako is naturally a border species, so it is ideal as an intermediary species between the garden and a natural forest boundary or a large established border planting; use it to break the line.

> • Large shrub 3–4 m
> • Full sun to semi-shade
> • Wind tolerant
> • Wet tolerant
> • Frost hardy

Brachyglottis 'Sunshine' is often confused with *B. greyi* in cultivation, and very often sold as *B. greyi*, as the two are very similar. *Brachyglottis* 'Sunshine' is part of a group of *Brachyglottis* called the Dunedin hybrids. It is believed to be a hybrid of *B. compacta* x *laxifolia*. It forms a compact bush that can grow up to 1 m high and at least as wide. The leaves have a very dense grey tomentum on both sides, hence the very grey appearance of the bush. The bright yellow flowers that form in summer are daisy-like in appearance and can be up to 3 cm in diameter. At times clusters of flowers can almost cover the bush.

LIKES AND DISLIKES: Dry soil conditions are very important since, like almost all *Brachyglottis* species, *B.* 'Sunshine' is very susceptible to *Phytophthora*. In very windy conditions the habit will be even more compact and the growth rate slower, but apart from that the effect will be minimal. It likes full sun to light shade, and in general will flower better in higher light levels. Many species of *Brachyglottis* are difficult to grow in warm humid areas, but *B.* 'Sunshine' can be grown with moderate ease.

PESTS AND PROBLEMS: Wet soil conditions are the main problem, and once fungus has affected the plant it rarely recovers. Prune it back severely, transplant it and spray with a systemic fungicide.

Striking grey foliage of *Brachyglottis* 'Sunshine'

CARE AND MAINTENANCE:

If grown in light to medium shade, *Brachyglottis* 'Sunshine' will require some pruning to keep a good shape, especially in warmer areas that have a longer growing season. It responds well to pruning and will bud up again very quickly. Like all *Brachyglottis* species it is very susceptible to collar rot, so keep any mulch or compost well away from the base of the shrub.

As this is a hybrid, cuttings are the only method of cultivation. *Brachyglottis* species are notoriously difficult to grow from seed anyway.

Compact bush of *B.* 'Sunshine'

LANDSCAPING SUGGESTIONS: *Brachyglottis* 'Sunshine' is an excellent filler, with a potential spread of a metre or more. It can be planted in front of a large mixed planting, providing not only a break in colour but also an intermediary size before smaller herbaceous plants like *Libertia*, *Parahebe*, rengarenga and groundcovers. On the coast it can be a feature species for a low planting with *Xeronema*, dwarf flaxes, *Myosotidium* and *Chionochloa*. With its foliage colour and bright yellow flowers it would look equally at home in a cottage garden.

CULTIVARS AND SIMILAR SPECIES: *Brachyglottis* 'Otari Cloud' can form a rounded bush over 1 m tall and the yellow flowers can be semi-doubles. It does better in full sun and tends to lose its form more readily than *B.* 'Sunshine'.

Brachyglottis greyi is very similar but the leaves have wavy margins and join abruptly to the petiole rather than tapering as on *B.* 'Sunshine'. It is also smaller growing and less vigorous.

> - Shrub approximately
>   1 m tall x 1 m wide
> - Full sun to semi-shade
> - Dry hardy
> - Wet intolerant
> - Wind hardy
> - Frost hardy
> - Coastally hardy

Carmichaelia arenaria • PUNAKAIKI BROOM

Native brooms in general are underutilised in New Zealand gardens, despite being quite hardy and easy to grow. Punakaiki broom is a small species (1 m) which is ideal for even small city gardens. The branches are very fine and green, with a weeping habit, and the foliage is virtually non-existent, as is the case with many species of broom. This unusual form can provide an excellent contrast to more broad-leaved plants. An added bonus is that in late spring or early summer the plant can become covered with small flowers that appear to be a lavender colour. They actually have a deep purple centre with white petals that on closer inspection reveal fine dark purple striations. The seed pods that form afterwards are a dark red-brown.

Not surprisingly, Punakaiki broom occurs naturally on limestone rocks and sandy soils around Punakaiki, on the west coast of the South Island.

LIKES AND DISLIKES: Punakaiki broom is very hardy, tolerating full sun to semi-shade and the full blast of coastal winds. It does wonderfully in very dry situations, where it tends to be tighter in habit and smaller. The only things to avoid are damp spots and rabbits!

PESTS AND PROBLEMS: For some strange reason rabbits love native brooms and will eat them to ground level, leaving nothing but the shortest of short stumps. Apart from this problem Punakaiki broom is very easy to look after, although *Carmichaelia* species are susceptible to galls, or swellings on the branchlets. Ideally, cut the damaged material out and spray with a contact or systemic insecticide.

CARE AND MAINTENANCE: No special maintenance is required. If necessary prune the plant to shape it, but no fancy techniques are needed.

Propagation is usually by cuttings, as the seeds of broom can be difficult to germinate.

LANDSCAPING SUGGESTIONS: Where to begin? Try using Punakaiki broom for a small hedge, spacing the plants about 40 cm apart. Its dry-loving nature makes it a must for exposed coastal gardens where nothing else seems to grow. Its unusual habit will make it a feature anywhere, especially if there is room to let it grow unpruned. Try planting it with glossy-leaved plants like Chatham Island forget-me-not and *Coprosma repens* mixed in with *Pachystegia* and flaxes. Plant large groups of each, and mix in some native grasses if there is room. Punakaiki broom's small stature also means it can fit into all but the smallest of rockeries, where again it can provide a contrasting form. If planting it into a garden bed, put it with other dry-loving plants like *Pimelea prostrata*, native irises and dwarf flax cultivars, with a contrasting backdrop of larger glossy-leaved plants like *Pseudopanax lessonii*, *Coprosma repens* and *Griselinia lucida*.

> • Small shrub 1 m
>   high, 70–80 cm wide
> • Full sun to semi-shade
> • Dry hardy
> • Wind hardy
> • Frost tolerant
> • Coastally hardy

Kaka beak forms a shrub 2 m high x 2 m wide. The delicate light green foliage is similar to that of the kowhai, as is the shape of the light red beak-like flowers. It looks quite spectacular in spring when the plant is in full bloom, although the display is quite short-lived. The major disadvantage to kaka beak is that it requires a conscientious gardener to keep it looking its best, since it is very susceptible to leaf miner caterpillar and thrips, both of which have a devastating effect on the plant.

Kaka beak is very rare in the wild, only occurring naturally in one or two place in the north of New Zealand.

LIKES AND DISLIKES: Kaka beak prefers a dry site and will quickly go into decline in waterlogged soils. It is coastally hardy and will also tolerate windy sites inland. It forms its most compact habit in high light levels but will tolerate some shade, where it will become more open and the flowers will be

Kaka beak flowers

more prominent, hanging from the branches in large clusters. Kaka beak is quite frost tender.

PESTS AND PROBLEMS: From spring through to early autumn, keep an eye out for leaf miner caterpillars on the plant. The succulent new shoots will disappear first, then the caterpillars will move on to the older leaves, which will develop holes and/or runnels. If the caterpillars are left unchecked, they can eventually kill the plant. Spray it with a systemic insecticide as soon as the infection is spotted and prune out infected material. Kaka beak buds very readily so it can recover quickly from such attacks, especially if growing conditions are reasonable. Kaka beak is also susceptible to thrips, a sap-sucking insect that lives on the chlorophyll of plants. When a plant has thrips it loses colour and starts to look anaemic, just like a human without enough iron. Plants tend to be more susceptible to thrips when they are under stress, for example too wet or hungry. It is generally not lethal and the plant will grow out of it. If desired, it can be sprayed with an insecticide to speed recovery. In either case, feed the plant (with foliar food, compost or granules) and check that all other conditions are satisfactory.

CARE AND MAINTENANCE: Regular pruning is necessary to keep a tight kaka beak shrub.

The shoots tend to grow straight out until their tips are nipped, at which point the numerous buds in the leaf axils become active. Kaka beak can be shaped with a pair of hedge cutters, so no fancy pruning techniques need to be learnt. Check regularly for pests.

The two most common methods of propagation are cuttings and seed; both are equally effective.

LANDSCAPING SUGGESTIONS: Kaka beak is a wonderful addition to any garden and can be pruned to fit whatever space is available; it can even be trained into a standard with a little bit of work. Instead of having a row of 'Iceberg' roses down either side of a path, how about a row of standard kaka beaks? The rapid growth rate of kaka beak makes it ideal for a new garden, where it can quickly bring structure to the often-barren landscape. In a small garden, it could

Clianthus puniceus 'Albus'

be positioned in a corner and act as a backdrop to smaller shrubs and herbaceous plants such as rengarenga, *Heliohebe*, *Libertia* and groundcover coprosmas. On the coast it could be left unpruned to wander through a shrubbery of flaxes, *Pseudopanax*, *Olearia lineata*, taupata and manuka. In addition to the spectacular red-flowering forms, try the white-flowering ones which are more subtle and add elegance to a planting that the red-flowering forms cannot.

CULTIVARS AND VARIETIES:
• *Clianthus puniceus* 'Albus' has very subtle pale green to white flowers. It is otherwise identical to *C. puniceus*.
• *Clianthus puniceus* 'Roseus' (syn. *C. puniceus* 'Flamingo') has rosy pink flowers.
• *Clianthus puniceus* var. *maximus* is even more striking in appearance than *C. puniceus*, with its bolder, larger, dark green foliage and its deeper-coloured flowers. Commercially, this is available as *Clianthus* 'Kaka King'.

- Shrub 2 m tall x 2 m wide
- Full sun to semi-shade
- Dry or free-draining site
- Wet intolerant
- Wind tolerant
- Frost tender
- Coastally hardy

These small-leaved coprosmas all grow to 1–2 m in height but vary in colour. While they could be considered fillers, many have beauty and structure in their own right. The following selection are all of a good habit and are also hardy, an important consideration when choosing a cultivar as many look good but are disease prone and/or have very specific requirements.

Coprosma 'Beatson's Gold'

LIKES AND DISLIKES: These cultivars will all tolerate moderately dry, free-draining conditions and are intolerant of wet conditions, especially in areas prone to humidity. Exposure will only improve the tightness of the plant's habit, as will full sun.

PESTS AND PROBLEMS: There are no major pests or problems with any of these cultivars.

Coprosma 'Karo Red'

CARE AND MAINTENANCE: All these cultivars will tolerate pruning and respond relatively quickly, especially on new growth. Mulch and compost will produce a healthier plant.

LANDSCAPING SUGGESTIONS: Small-leaved coprosmas are almost divaricating in their form. Although the branches do not interweave they do tend to be very closely spaced, creating dense shrubs. They all look good with large glossy-leaved species, and with grasses and groundcovers. They can also be mixed together and planted en masse, looking like an artist's palette after a day's work. The smaller-leaved, tighter forms could be topiaried, and any of them could be planted to form a low-growing hedge.

CULTIVARS:

• *Coprosma* 'Beatson's Brown' syn. *C.* 'Beatson's Bronze' has small bronze leaves and grows 1–2 m tall.

• *Coprosma* 'Beatson's Gold' has small green and yellow variegated leaves. It forms a dense shrub of 1–2 m, spreading horizontally and vertically at the same time.

• *Coprosma* 'Cutie' has lovely small glossy leaves that are a dark chocolate colour, becoming dark green, rimmed with dark brown, through the growing season. It has an upright habit and grows to 1–2 m.

• *Coprosma* 'Greensleeves' also has an upright habit, and grows to 1–2 m. The leaves are bright green and slightly linear in form.

• *Coprosma* 'Karo Red' has foliage that changes colour with the seasons, like *C.* 'Cutie', but the leaves are larger at 15–25 mm and the coloration is more a dark red. It has a compact habit but can spread more horizontally than vertically. It grows to 1 m in height.

• *Coprosma* 'Katie Reynolds' is very similar to *C.* 'Beatson's Brown', with small glossy dark green and brown leaves. The branches can almost form tiers like a beech tree. It grows 1.5–2 m tall.

• *Coprosma* 'Middlemore' is like a green-leaved form of *C.* 'Cutie' but is bushier in its habit.

> • Shrubs 1–2 m tall
> • Full sun to semi-shade
> • Dry tolerant
> • Wind hardy
> • Frost tolerant
> • OK in coastal
>   plantings

Taupata's classic thick dark shiny green leaves have been used as the base for many a cultivar. As a species it can vary a lot in habit, from a shrub of 3 m or more to an almost prostrate ground-cover, and all forms in between. The prostrate forms tend to be sold as *Coprosma repens* 'Prostrate Form' or *C. repens* 'Poor Knights' as distinct from *C.* 'Prostrata', which is thought to be a hybrid between taupata and *C. kirkii.* The leaves of the taupata are 5–9 cm long x 3–7 cm wide and can be curled under on the margins. The flowers are inconspicuous on the separate male and female plants, but the female bears orange to red fruit that the birds love.

Taupata hedge

Taupata occurs throughout the North Island, to Greymouth on the west coast of the South Island and Marlborough on the east.

LIKES AND DISLIKES: Taupata is tolerant of very exposed, dry conditions but does not like waterlogged or wet soil. It will tolerate light shade but in deeper shade will tend to lose its form and become very stretched. It is tolerant of only very light frosts.

PESTS AND PROBLEMS: In wet conditions taupata is susceptible to *Phytophthora*, visible as a yellowing of the leaves, which will also lose their gloss. In warm humid areas taupata can be prone to black spot and rust; the former can be dealt with by spraying with a fungicide and the latter with copper oxychloride. These diseases can be minimised by planting taupata in an exposed position.

CARE AND MAINTENANCE: In warmer areas, where the growth rate will be more vigorous, pruning may be necessary to keep a good shape. In exposed positions this should not be necessary. If the leaves become more yellow in colour and the plant is not too wet, feed it. Taupata is prone to collar rot so keep mulch and compost well away from the trunk.

Propagation is by cuttings or seed, but as it hybridises readily cuttings are better, unless the plant is growing on its own with no other *Coprosma* species around.

LANDSCAPING SUGGESTIONS: In very exposed sites taupata can form some interesting, almost sculptural, shapes; for me, this is taupata at its best. However, for the ultimate in orderliness, it can also be formed into a clipped hedge. On the coast it could be planted with species like *Astelia banksii*, Chatham Island forget-me-not, flaxes and cabbage trees, with grasses scattered in amongst them. Taupata can look equally good in a garden situation, as a backdrop for grey-foliaged and divaricating plants whose forms will be accentuated by its glossy green. Some forms of taupata can have a lovely weeping habit; these can be trained to a single-leader form for the first 1–2 m of their height then left to cascade down, creating an umbrella-like plant.

Coprosma repens 'Marble Queen'

Summer foliage of *Coprosma repens* 'Yvonne'

CULTIVARS:

• *Coprosma repens* 'Marble Queen' has attractive leaves with irregular white margins and speckles. It can be so speckled with white that it appears more white than green. Since it has less chlorophyll it tends to have a slower growth rate but consequently has a good habit. Smaller growing at 1–2 m.

• *Coprosma repens* 'Painter's Palette' has cream, red, yellow, green and chocolate variegations, with the colours intensifying in winter. Smaller growing at 1–2 m.

• *Coprosma repens* 'Picturata' has leaves that are irregularly marked with cream and yellow green in the centre, leaving an irregular green margin. Smaller growing at 1–2 m.

• *Coprosma repens* 'Silver Queen' has a fine creamy white margin to the leaves. 2–3 m in height.

• *Coprosma repens* 'Variegata' is very similar to *C. repens* 'Silver Queen' but is more yellow in its variegation.

• *Coprosma repens* 'Yvonne' has dark green to chocolate-coloured leaves, which turn a deep red-bronze colour in winter. Grows to 2 m.

> • Shrub averaging 3 m tall
> • Full sun to semi-shade
> • Dry tolerant
> • Wet intolerant
> • Wind hardy
> • Frost tender
> • Coastally hardy

Coprosma rhamnoides is a divaricating species that can form some interesting shapes, especially in very exposed positions in full sun. It is perhaps seen at its best on wind-swept hillsides where these forms can merge into those of manuka. It has small round pale to olive-green leaves that occur on fine pale brown branches that can arch towards the ground. It forms a shrub that can grow to 3 m, but moderately slowly. The female plants have deep red to black berries that hang in the plant like small rubies and are slightly sweet to eat.

Coprosma rhamnoides is found throughout New Zealand in scrubland through to lower montane forests.

LIKES AND DISLIKES: *Coprosma rhamnoides* is very tolerant of dry conditions but less so of wet. It prefers full sun but will tolerate shade, and salt-laden air is not a problem. A very hardy species!

PESTS AND PROBLEMS: There are no major pests or problems.

CARE AND MAINTENANCE: *Coprosma rhamnoides* can be left to grow with no care and attention, but it can also be pruned if you wish to alter its shape. It can take time to resprout from old wood, however, and if it is not growing vigorously, it may not do so. Mulch and/or compost will help to keep it healthy and green, but avoid the trunk. Remember, too, that poorer conditions will probably produce a more interesting stunted plant.

LANDSCAPING SUGGESTIONS: *Coprosma rhamnoides* is ideal as an underplanting species, where it could be planted with kawakawa, *Carex dissita*, *Libertia*, rengarenga, turutu and *Asplenium oblongifolium*. On the coast it could provide a contrast in a planting of *Pseudopanax lessonii*, ngaio, Chatham Island forget-me-not, *Heliohebe hulkeana* and *Fuchsia procumbens*. Although its growth rate is relatively slow it could be used for topiary, but you would need to start when the plant was still quite young as the younger growth responds better to pruning. In this form it could be a feature of a simple low garden with *Muehlenbeckia axillaris* and *Libertia peregrinans*. Or, for a more formal look, *Coprosma rhamnoides* could be shaped into 'lollipops' and planted either side of a pathway with *Pimelea prostrata* as a groundcover; if the plants had clear trunks of 70 cm or so, a bed of *Carex albula* could form the groundcover.

CULTIVARS:
• *Coprosma* 'Mangatangi' is a selected form of *C. rhamnoides*. It has a very compact habit and is small growing at only 75 cm. Its overall appearance is like a pale green hedgehog.

> • Shrub 2–3 m tall
> • Full sun to shade
> • Dry tolerant
> • Wind hardy
> • Frost hardy
> • Coastally hardy

The divaricating habit of *Coprosma rhamnoides*

The compact form of *Coprosma* 'Mangatangi'

Hedge of *Coprosma virescens*

Coprosma virescens

The most endearing things about *Coprosma virescens* are its fine tangly habit, orange branches and delicate green leaves. *Fact time: The tangly habit in plants is often referred to as a 'divaricating habit'. New Zealand, in comparative terms, abounds in such plants. There is some debate as to why this is; one of the many theories is that the plants evolved like this as a protection against the browsing of moa.* Some people dislike the form of divaricating plants, but they often provide a useful contrast. If a divaricating species is planted next to a species with bold tropical foliage, both are enhanced. The small, contained stature of *Coprosma virescens* (2 m high x 1 m wide) means it will fit easily into a small city garden.

Coprosma virescens occurs naturally in lowland forest and forest margins from the Kaimanawa Ranges south.

LIKES AND DISLIKES: Like many of the *Coprosma* species this one has very few dislikes. It will tolerate exposed dry windy sites, semi-shade or full sun and even quite poor soils, but it will grow most vigorously if planted in a free-draining soil with adequate moisture. Wet soils and deep shade are the only conditions that should be avoided.

PESTS AND PROBLEMS: *Coprosma virescens* is pest free and has no real problems.

CARE AND MAINTENANCE: With its divaricating habit *Coprosma virescens* can form a variety of interesting shapes, like a naturally evolving sculpture. The shape of the plant can be moulded to your own design as *Coprosma virescens* responds well to pruning on younger wood. Feed and mulch it well to achieve optimum growth rates, avoiding contact with the bark.

Cuttings are the usual means of propagation. Seed can be used, but make sure there are no other coprosmas nearby as they hybridise quite readily.

LANDSCAPING SUGGESTIONS: This species looks good and grows well in most situations. It can be planted as a specimen amid groundcovers and grasses, either singly or in a small group, or it can be planted close to bold-foliaged plants such as *Pseudopanax laetus* or the vine *Tecomanthe speciosa*. *Coprosma virescens* can form a wonderful, slightly informal hedge if left to grow at will. Another option is to plant it around the base of the erect, sculptural forms of lancewood and/or cabbage trees. Its relative tolerance to dryness also makes it an ideal pot plant.

- Shrub 2 m tall, up to 1 m wide
- Full sun to semi-shade
- Dry tolerant
- Wind tolerant
- Frost hardy
- Tolerates coastal conditions

Corokia cotoneaster is another divaricating shrub, with wonderful fine black branches. It grows to a height of 1–3 m although, like most divaricating plants, it is slow to gain height but is very dense. *Corokia cotoneaster* has very small leaves that can be variable in shape but are quite insignificant in the overall appearance of the plant; the new growth can at times appear entirely leafless. Like all *Corokia* species and cultivars, *C. cotoneaster* has small bright yellow flowers that hang like stars within the body of the plant. These flowers later transform into red or yellow fruit 5–8 mm in diameter which can hang on the shrub for many months.

Corokia cotoneaster occurs throughout New Zealand on river flats, rocky places and lowland scrubland to 760 m. In the South Island it does not occur west of the alps.

LIKES AND DISLIKES: Avoid planting in areas that can have high moisture levels. Very dry sites are completely tolerable, although the growth rate will be a lot slower. It will tolerate full sun through to semi-shade, and very exposed situations.

PESTS AND PROBLEMS: There are no major pests or problems.

CARE AND MAINTENANCE: *Corokia cotoneaster* can be pruned to shape and responds readily. Composting and mulching regularly will benefit the plant's health, but avoid contact with the trunk.

Both seed and cuttings are used for propagation. The cuttings are semi-hardwood so can take time to develop roots, but are generally very successful. The seed

Compact form of *Corokia cotoneaster*

Corokia x *virgata* 'Frosted Chocolate'

is surrounded by a very hard seedcase that can delay germination.

Dark red fruit of *Corokia*

LANDSCAPING SUGGESTIONS: *Corokia cotoneaster* can add contrast and variety in a garden, and can even be used in a bromeliad planting where it would add height and a different texture. Its tight divaricating habit makes it ideal as a hedging species, especially in exposed sites, and it could even be trained into a medium-sized 'box' hedge. Try it in a mixed planting with *Olearia*, *Pseudopanax*, *Asplenium oblongifolium* and rengarenga, and in a coastal planting combine it with hebes, *Chionochloa*, *Pachystegia*, *Brachyglottis* and rengarenga. It might be used to underplant whau or kowhai, or in a rock garden it could be the feature plant in the company of *Scleranthus*, *Linum*, *Astelia banksii*, Chatham Island forget-me-not and *Acaena inermis* 'Purpurea'.

Yellow flowers of *Corokia*

CULTIVARS:
• *Corokia cotoneaster* 'Little Prince' has smaller leaves and a more upright habit.
The following are all *Corokia* x *virgata* cultivars:
• 'Bronze King' has fine bronze-coloured foliage that averages 1.5 cm long x 6 mm wide, and grows to a height of 2 m.
• 'Cheesmanii' is similar to 'Bronze King' but green in colour. It is a prolific flowerer and has red fruit.
• 'Frosted Chocolate' has brown foliage that becomes more intense in winter. The leaves are 2.5–5 cm x 1–1.7 cm. It grows to a height of 2–3 m.
• 'Geentys Green' has bright green leaves and a very compact habit. It is slightly smaller, at 1–1.5 m.
• 'Red Wonder' is very similar to 'Cheesmanii' with its bright red berries but is more erect.
• 'Sunsplash' is the only variegated *Corokia* commonly in cultivation. The variegation is cream and grey green, and it grows to 1–1.5 m.
• 'Yellow Wonder' has a very branching habit and is denser than some of the other cultivars. It has larger leaves and abundant bright yellow fruit.

• Shrub 1–3 m tall
• Full sun to semi-shade
• Dry tolerant
• Wind hardy
• Frost hardy
• OK in coastal gardens

Entelea arborescens • WHAU

Whau is sometimes referred to as New Zealand's 'cork tree' as the wood is very light; when dried it is only half the weight of cork. It is very fast growing, quick to attain height and width, and forms a large shrub 3–4 m tall with a lovely spreading habit. The soft heart-shaped leaves are very large and a pale spring green. Their softness means they hang from the plant or float in the wind like round green pennants. In spring and early summer the plant can be festooned with clusters of white flowers about 2.5 cm in diameter. In summer the flowers transform themselves into a spiny fruit not unlike a chestnut burr.

Whau occurs coastally and in open lowland forests in the North Island to the Bay of Plenty in the east and Raglan in the west. It is also very localised in the Nelson and Marlborough areas.

LIKES AND DISLIKES: Frost and high moisture levels are whau's main dislikes. It prefers a free-draining soil, and is tolerant of full sun through to semi-shade. Strangely, in view of its soft leaves, whau is tolerant of coastal conditions.

PESTS AND PROBLEMS: Whau is virtually problem and pest free.

CARE AND MAINTENANCE: Ensure whau is planted somewhere not too wet and not too dry, although it will tolerate a degree of dryness. The leaves may wilt but the plant seems to recover

The spiny fruit of whau with a few flowers visible

fairly readily when conditions come right. In dry areas make sure the plant is well mulched in spring when the ground is still wet, so that it retains this moisture. As always, make sure the mulch does not touch the trunk of the tree. Pruning can be done at any time, but whau responds more quickly if pruned during a growing season.

If large numbers of plants are required, seed is by far the easiest method of propagation, but cuttings can also be taken with moderate success.

LANDSCAPING SUGGESTIONS: On the coast whau can provide shelter relatively quickly yet still look lush. It also has the added bonus of being a prolific flowerer, unlike many large coastal shrubs. It could be planted as a hedge line, on its own or among other species like *Olearia*, *Griselinia lucida* and kowhai. With judicious pruning from an early age it could form a small shade tree, its open habit providing dappled light for the plants underneath. Underplant it with species like Chatham Island forget-me-not, astelias, kaka beak and rengarenga.

- Shrub 3–4 m tall
- Full sun to semi-shade
- Dry tolerant
- Wet intolerant
- Wind tolerant
- Frost intolerant
- OK in coastal gardens

A large compact shrub of whau in full bloom beside a karaka

Hebe cultivars

Hebes are a wonderful group of plants, with huge variations in leaf form and colour, plant habit and size, and in flower colour, size and flowering time. There is just about a species or cultivar to fit any description, although finding it could be more difficult. Each nursery can only grow a certain number of hebes, but if you can't find the one you are looking for, don't worry; there will be another very similar one that will fill the space just as well.

LIKES AND DISLIKES: Hebes prefer a dry, free-draining position as they are prone to root rot. They are tolerant of exposure and some, especially the large-leaved hebes, are less disease prone in such situations. Exposure keeps the humidity levels down, creating an environment that is less conducive to fungal development. All hebes prefer full sun and many will tolerate light shade; as the shade levels increase the plant will become more stretched and require more regular pruning to keep a tight habit.

PESTS AND PROBLEMS: It is best to prune hebes from spring through to early autumn, as pruning later can give rise to downy mildew, resulting in distorted new growth which can take the plant many months to recover from. Black spot, a fungal disease, is more common on large-leaved hebes, especially in warm humid climates. Both these diseases can be treated with a fungicide. Another common problem is what is called Veronica gallery fly, which eats the new young buds resulting in a hebe with holey foliage. This can be treated with a systemic insecticide, or prune off the infected foliage; it is advisable to cut off any infected material regardless of the disease.

CARE AND MAINTENANCE: While most species of hebe require some maintenance they are not difficult to look after. Keep an eye out for fungal problems, and prune your hebe regularly. Most require pruning once or twice a year, depending on the species and where you live. Try and leave foliage on a pruned branch so that it will bud more readily; if there is no foliage, the branch may not bud at all and may die. Hebes will show if they require feeding through a yellowing of the leaves and a loss of plant vigour; this will vary from species to species.

Cuttings are the preferred method of propagation as hebes are notoriously difficult to grow from seed. The young seedlings are very prone to fungal attack, which can whip through a seed tray in a matter of days. The other problem is finding a pure seed source, as hebes hybridise quite readily. Cuttings take very easily and purity is assured. For cultivars, cuttings are the only means of propagation.

LANDSCAPING SUGGESTIONS: As long as there is a moderate amount of sun and the soil does not become too wet, there is a hebe to suit most landscaping situations. There are grey-foliaged forms through to dark green; thin, matt leaves to thick glossy leaves; prostrate forms to those that grow to 1.5 m or more and white flowers through to deep magenta and all colours in between. Hebes will do very well in a pot, either by themselves or with other species, and they can look great with grasses, whether it be large grass and small hebe or vice versa. Hebes are excellent on the coast, where they can be very low maintenance; the exposure not only keeps fungal problems to a minimum but encourages a tight habit .

CULTIVARS:

WHITE
H. 'Snowdrift' (1 m)
H. 'Wiri Mist' (30 cm x 1 m)

PALE TO DEEP PINK
H. 'Anne' (1 m+)
H 'Eveline' (1 m)
H. 'First Light' (30 cm x 90 cm)
H. 'Icing Sugar' (75 cm x 1 m)
H. 'Mary Antoinette' (75 cm)
H. 'Oratia Beauty' (75 cm x 1 m)
H. 'Wiri Cloud' (40–50 cm)
H. 'Wiri Dawn' (45 cm x 1 m)
H. 'Wiri Gem' (90 cm)
H. 'Wiri Port' (90 cm)

PALE TO DEEP LAVENDER
H. 'Champagne' (50 cm x 90 cm)
H. 'Hartii' (10 cm x 75 cm) [[10 cm?]]
H. 'Lavender Lace' (1–1.5 m)
H. 'McEwanii' (50 cm)
H. 'Wiri Grace' (1.5 m)

REDS AND PURPLES
H. 'Autumn Glory' (50 cm)
H. 'Inspiration' (up to 1 m)
H. 'Inveray' (prostrate)
H. 'La Séduisante' (1 m)
H. pimeleoides 'Quicksilver' (30 cm)
H. 'Wiri Charm' (75 cm x 1.3 m)
H. 'Wiri Image' (1 m)
H. 'Wiri Prince' (1 m)
H. 'Wiri Splash' (50 cm x 70 cm)
H. 'Wiri Vision' (90 cm x 1.2 m)

• *Hebe* 'Anne' is derived from *H. speciosa*. It has glossy green leaves and produces 9 cm spikes of rich pink flowers for long periods, particularly in winter.

• *Hebe* 'Autumn Glory' is a small shrub with dark green leaves and short spikes of violet flowers in summer through to autumn.

• *Hebe* 'Champagne' is a low-growing shrub with dark green leaves that are flushed with purple. In late summer it bears pale violet to white flowers. A useful groundcover plant and good in containers.

• *Hebe* 'Emerald Gem' syn. 'Emerald Green' is a low, bun-shaped plant 20–30 cm tall, with attractive fresh green semi-whipcord foliage.

• *Hebe* 'Eveline' is a rounded shrub that resembles *H. speciosa*. In summer it bears long spikes of deep pink flowers. Prone to fungal diseases such as black spot, it is best in a sunny, open site. Good for coastal planting.

• *Hebe* 'First Light', named for the new millennium, forms a low spreading shrub with fleshy green leaves that are bronzed when young. Short crowded racemes of pink flowers are borne over a prolonged period. Suitable for growing in containers.

• *Hebe* x *franciscana* 'Variegata' syn. *H.* 'Waireka' is a variegated shrub with creamy yellow leaf margins and purple flowers in summer.

• *Hebe* 'Hartii' has small glossy green leaves and 5 cm spikes of pale mauve flowers that appear in profusion in spring. It is a very useful groundcover that will spill over walls and banks.

• *Hebe* 'Icing Sugar' bears racemes of pink flowers for a long period in late summer, the flowers

Hebe 'Wiri Prince'

Hebe 'Wiri Charm'

Hebe 'Wiri Port'

Hebe 'First Light'

gradually fading to white, giving a two-toned effect. It is best in sunny open areas and good in containers.

• *Hebe* 'Inspiration' is a popular plant that has dark green shiny leaves and purple flowers that appear throughout the year, although the main flowering period is during summer. Trim after flowering to encourage further flushes and keep the plant tidy. Good for coastal areas.

• *Hebe* 'Inveray' is a prostrate plant with grey foliage and deep purple flowers in summer. It is very cold hardy, is suitable for rock gardens and good in containers.

• *Hebe* 'La Séduisante' is an old hybrid with *H. speciosa* parentage. The large leaves are shiny dark green with purplish undersides, edges and midribs. Rich purple-red flowers occur during summer and intermittently until early winter.

• *Hebe* 'Lavender Lace' has narrow light green leaves and racemes of lavender flowers, fading to white, from early summer to early winter. It is a very free-flowering and easy-care plant.

• *Hebe* 'McEwanii' is a compact shrub with small narrow glaucous leaves on purplish stems. Pale mauve flowers in summer.

• *Hebe* 'Mary Antoinette' has leaves that are an attractive reddish bronze when new, ageing to olive green. The flowers, borne in summer and autumn, are cerise fading to pink and white. Its name is not a misspelling of the famous queen but a combination of names of staff at the nursery where it arose.

• *Hebe ochracea* 'James Stirling' is a whipcord species with tiny scale-like leaves that are an attractive rich golden colour. Better in cooler areas.

• *Hebe* 'Oratia Beauty' is a very popular plant that forms a compact shrub with fleshy deep green leaves and racemes of pink flowers, fading to white, in summer and autumn.

• *Hebe pimeleoides* 'Quicksilver' is a low-spreading shrub with small bluish grey leaves and purplish blue flowers in summer. It is an excellent groundcover for rock gardens, and a good container plant. Prefers well-drained conditions and does better in cooler areas.

• *Hebe* 'Snowdrift' is a neat shrub with light green leaves. It bears masses of white flowers in early summer and again in winter to spring.

HEBE: THE 'WIRI' SERIES

These hebes have resulted from a breeding programme at the Auckland Regional Botanic Gardens. They make attractive garden subjects and have a variety of forms and colours.

• *Hebe* 'Wiri Charm' is a relatively compact shrub if pruned regularly, and has undulating foliage. Deep rose-purple flowers are borne in summer with a lesser flush in winter. Good in containers.

• *Hebe* 'Wiri Cloud' requires regular pruning to keep its form but it does become covered in small pink flowers in summer. It is a good rock-garden plant and also suitable for containers. Cold hardy.

Hebe 'Inspiration'

• *Hebe* 'Wiri Dawn' has pale olive-green foliage that contrasts with the pale pinkish white flowers for long periods in summer and again in autumn and winter. Makes a good container plant and will spill attractively over a wall.

• *Hebe* 'Wiri Gem' has rose-pink flowers borne near the branch tips for up to nine months of the year, the main period being autumn to spring.

• *Hebe* 'Wiri Grace' is a vigorously growing shrub with long spikes of lavender flowers in summer.

• *Hebe* 'Wiri Image' is a vigorous yet neat shrub with fresh green foliage and violet flowers in early summer.

• *Hebe* 'Wiri Mist' is a spreading shrub that bears masses of white flowers from late spring. Maintains a compact form without clipping and is very easy-care, making it suitable for mass planting and low-maintenance areas.

• *Hebe* 'Wiri Port' is a compact shrub with dense racemes of flowers that are an unusual pinkish wine shade. Can be frost tender, and prone to leaf spot in sheltered situations.

• *Hebe* 'Wiri Prince' has dark green leaves and long racemes of rich purple flowers in winter and again in summer.

• *Hebe* 'Wiri Splash' is a dense shrub with small yellowish green foliage and a single flush of lilac flowers in early summer. It is a good disease-resistant plant for areas of high humidity and also cold hardy.

• *Hebe* 'Wiri Vision' is a vigorous shrub with a rather open habit that can be tightened with regular pruning. Reddish purple flowers appear abundantly in summer.

*H*ebe *diosmifolia* is but one of many pure species of *Hebe*, but it has been widely used in hybridisation because of its hardiness. As a species it can vary greatly in form, from a low-growing bush of only 40 cm to an upright shrub of 1.5 m or more. The leaves all have fine teeth or notches and are linear in form. The small lavender to white flowers are borne in much-branched clusters, forming flowering heads that can cover the plant in spring. A second flowering will often occur in late summer or early autumn.

Hebe diosmifolia has localised populations throughout the northern part of Northland, often with slight differences between each population.

LIKES AND DISLIKES: *Hebe diosmifolia* will tolerate quite a lot of shade while still maintaining its form. It is tolerant of coastal conditions but will not tolerate high moisture levels in the soil, being susceptible to *Phytophthora*.

PESTS AND PROBLEMS: See *Hebe* Cultivars.

CARE AND MAINTENANCE: *Hebe diosmifolia* requires little maintenance. It is not a gross feeder and will tolerate quite poor soils, but if the leaves start to yellow and it is not too wet, feed it! It

Hebe diosmifolia in full flower

has a readily branching habit so requires minimal pruning to keep a good form, although it can be pruned to whatever shape you like, even a standard. See 'Hebe cultivars' for further information.

LANDSCAPING SUGGESTIONS: When buying your *Hebe diosmifolia* make sure it is going to grow to the height you want; there is no point in getting a form that will grow to 1.5 m when you only have room for a very small plant. The dwarf form, which has much darker leaves and can be almost covered in flowers in spring and autumn, is ideal for a small rockery or on the edge of a cottage garden. Large groups can be planted with Poor Knights lily and *Astelia* acting as specimens. The taller forms tend to do very well in semi-shaded situations, keeping their habit and still flowering well, so are good as an underplanting for established vegetation or on a shaded side of the house. *Hebe diosmifolia* could even be the dominant species in a bed of grasses, with small groups scattered through the planting.

CULTIVARS:
• *Hebe diosmifolia* 'Garden Beauty' has slightly longer leaves and a habit that is a little more lax. The new branches are an attractive red that contrasts with the deep green leaves.
• *Hebe diosmifolia* 'Wairua Beauty' is thought to be more floriferous with larger flower heads. It has a more erect habit than *H. diosmifolia* 'Garden Beauty'.

> • Small shrub
>   40 cm–2 m tall
> • Full sun to light shade
> • Dry tolerant
> • Wind tolerant
> • Frost tolerant
> • OK coastally

*H*ebe macrocarpa var. *macrocarpa*, as it is more correctly known, is very similar to koromiko, or *Hebe stricta*. The most obvious difference is that its large leaves are much fleshier. The colour of the leaves can vary from spring green to dark green. It is a fast-growing plant and if left to establish on its own, will reach around 1.5 m in height. It has an upright habit and although it will tolerate some shade this does tend to emphasise its erect habit; it will be bushier in full sun. The flowers form in long white racemes sporadically through much of the year. In cultivation, especially in the warm north, *Hebe macrocarpa* is less prone to black spot and other common *Hebe* diseases than *H. stricta*.

Hebe macrocarpa is found in the upper part of the North Island in disturbed or open country.

LIKES AND DISLIKES: See *Hebe* Cultivars.

PESTS AND PROBLEMS: Although *Hebe macrocarpa* is more forgiving of wet and/or humid conditions than many large-leaved *Hebe* species, it is still susceptible to fungal attack by both powdery mildew and black spot. See '*Hebe* cultivars' for further information.

CARE AND MAINTENANCE: See *Hebe* Cultivars.

LANDSCAPING SUGGESTIONS: *Hebe macrocarpa* has a more vigorous growth rate than many species of *Hebe* and can be used in areas where quick establishment is important. Its floriferous habit makes it ideal as a marginal species between long-established vegetation and 'garden planting'. It could be planted with *Astelia* species, makomako, flaxes, *Muehlenbeckia astonii* and native grasses. As with many species of *Hebe*, its flowering habit earns it a tick!

VARIETIES: *Hebe macrocarpa* var. *latisepala* has even fleshier leaves than *H. macrocarpa* and they are darker green. The flowers are a deep purple-magenta colour, on a similar length flower spike. It will only tolerate light frosts.

- Shrub 1.5–2 m tall
- Full sun to semi-shade
- Dry tolerant
- Wind tolerant
- Frost tolerant
- OK in coastal gardens

Hebe parviflora

Hebe parviflora can range in height from 2 m to the size of a small tree, although most of the forms in cultivation are at the lower end of the range. This is another species of *Hebe* that requires minimal, if any, pruning. It has a well-branched habit and forms a tight bush if grown in full sun or even semi-shade. The leaves are a pale spring green colour and are small and linear in shape. It can take a few years to flower after planting, but once it does the long racemes of pale lavender-white flowers hang profusely on the plant in summer. This is an underutilised species of *Hebe* which is very hardy and low in maintenance. Unlike many species of *Hebe*, it is moderately tolerant of high moisture levels.

Hebe parviflora occurs throughout New Zealand from sea level to 600 m in scrublands, forest margins, streamsides and other open areas.

LIKES AND DISLIKES: See *Hebe* Cultivars.

PESTS AND PROBLEMS: See *Hebe* Cultivars.

CARE AND MAINTENANCE: See *Hebe* Cultivars.

LANDSCAPING SUGGESTIONS: *Hebe parviflora* can be used as a hedging plant; although not fast to gain height it requires no pruning to keep it dense. It is also ideal if the space is narrow as it can easily be pruned to fit. Its unusual pale green colour makes it a useful addition to large plantings with species such as *Corokia cotoneaster*, *Pseudopanax laetus* and *Olearia paniculata*, overtopped with *Hoheria sexstylosa* and *Nestegis montana*. It is also tolerant of semi-shaded situations where other hebes may become more open in their habit; in such sites it could be planted with *Polystichum vestitum*, *Mazus radicans*, *Xeronema* and rengarenga.

- Shrub approximately 2 m tall
- Full sun to semi-shade
- Dry tolerant
- Tolerant of moist situations
- Wind hardy
- Frost hardy
- OK in coastal gardens

VARIETIES: *Hebe parviflora* var. *arborea* is a taller-growing form that can reach 6 m in height. In cultivation the naming of these two species has become a little blurred, though most are the smaller-growing *H. parviflora*.

Hebe parviflora

Hebe speciosa

This is a striking *Hebe* that is much sought after. The leaves are a dark glossy green, oval in shape with an indented midrib. The margins of the leaves are often a deep magenta, as are the midrib and the young new stems. It forms a bush that can be a metre or more in height and an even greater width if it is left to develop uncontained, although it can easily be pruned to the desired size and shape. The flower spikes are very solid and a deep reddish purple colour that contrasts with the dark green of the leaves.

Hebe speciosa is very localised in its distribution, found only in pockets on the west coast of the North Island and only at Titirangi Bay in Pelorus Sound in the South Island.

LIKES AND DISLIKES: In northern parts of the country *Hebe speciosa* requires an exposed position, as it is very prone to fungal attack. See *Hebe* Cultivars for further information.

PESTS AND PROBLEMS: See *Hebe* Cultivars.

CARE AND MAINTENANCE: *Hebe speciosa* responds well to regular pruning, which is often necessary to maintain a tight habit, especially in warmer climates where the growth rate can be more vigorous. Pruning should take precedence over flowering for the first year or so while the overall plant shape is developing. Keep a close eye out for fungal infections and deal with them promptly. See *Hebe* Cultivars for further information.

LANDSCAPING SUGGESTIONS: *Hebe speciosa* is ideal in exposed coastal conditions, where fungal problems are kept to a minimum and the growth rate is slower, creating a denser plant which requires less maintenance. In such situations it could be planted with *Olearia lineata*, karo, *Pachystegia*, *Astelia* species, *Chionochloa* and coastal grasses. It also suits large rockeries or exposed banks, where it could be planted with astelias, rengarenga, *Hebe parviflora*, *Linum* and flaxes. Since it will tolerate some shade without becoming too stretched, *Hebe speciosa* can be used under open trees like whau and kowhai, or under large specimen trees like titoki and silver beech.

CULTIVARS:
• *Hebe speciosa* 'Dobbies Delight' is a selected form from Maunganui Bluff that is less disease prone than other forms, especially in areas with high humidity. The leaves are a little lighter in colour and lack the magenta coloration found in some forms.

• Shrub 1–1.5 m tall
• Full sun to semi-shade
• Dry tolerant
• Wet intolerant
• Wind hardy
• Tolerates light frosts
• Coastally hardy

This is probably one of the most common species in New Zealand, covering a large portion of the scrubland and often being one of the first species to come back after land disturbance. Manuka is very fast growing and quickly forms a large shrub. If left unattended as an individual specimen, it will tend to be quite bushy, though still forming a short clear trunk. In a mass planting the clear trunk will tend to be taller, but it is not classically a single-leader tree. In cultivation manuka grows to a height of 3–5 m. The leaves are very small and feel quite prickly to the touch, especially on slightly older plants. The white flowers are approximately 12 mm in diameter and occur sporadically between September and June

Manuka occurs throughout New Zealand from sea level to subalpine areas, generally in what is, or once was, open country.

Flowers of *Leptospermum* 'Red Damask'

LIKES AND DISLIKES: Manuka is a very tolerant species. It will tolerate very wet conditions through to very dry, although with the extremes of conditions it is considered better to plant like into like, i.e., plant seed collected from wet-area plants into wet areas, and seed from dry areas into dry. Manuka is also very tolerant of wind exposure, and in such conditions some interesting forms can be created. Shady conditions are outside its tolerance limits and should be avoided.

PESTS AND PROBLEMS: The honeydew-secreting insect that lives in cracks in the bark of manuka is the main pest. Sooty mould lives on this secretion and slowly smothers the leaves, covering all but the very outside ones. It can be lethal on manuka but tends not to be so on kanuka, which is not affected to the same extent. One solution is to apply a mixture of summer oil and contact insecticide, ensuring that the branches on the inside of the plant and around the base are coated with spray. This should be done twice a year, once in spring and once in autumn. Sooty mould is much less of a problem in inner city gardens, but on the outskirts or near scrublands it can be a major problem and vigilance will be necessary to keep your plants healthy. The only other problem is a type of caterpillar that forms a web, binding shoots together; the affected branches can be pruned out.

CARE AND MAINTENANCE: If your manuka requires pruning, do it judiciously, as it only readily buds from the new growth; it buds very slowly if at all from old wood.

The main means of propagation for pure manuka is seed, which tends to take very readily. For cultivars, propagation is by cuttings.

LANDSCAPING SUGGESTIONS: Its hardiness, fine foliage and floriferous nature make manuka a fine addition to any garden. The pure manuka tends to be more upright than many of the bushier cultivars, and hence it can make a wonderful small shade tree that is very fast growing. A small grove could be planted in the corner of a garden with low-growing *Carex* species forming a carpet underneath, or manuka could be part of a mixed border with cabbage trees, lancewoods, mapou and *Pseudopanax laetus*. Around a dam it could be planted with cabbage trees, ribbonwood, harakeke, *Carex secta* and *Astelia grandis*, with *Gunnera prorepens* meandering through.

CULTIVARS:
KEY: (S) = single flower; (D) = double flower; measurement is height; season is flowering time.

WHITE
• 'Karekare': (S), 2 m, spring
• 'Princess Anne': (D), 2 m, summer, dark maroon centre
• 'Snow Flurry': (D), 1.5 m, spring to mid-summer, white with a touch of crimson, upright habit
• 'Wiri Linda': (D), 1.7 m, early autumn and spring
• 'Wiri Susan': (S), 1.2 m, spring, large flowers

PINKS
• 'Autumn Glory': (S), 2 m, spring, bushy habit

Leptospermum 'Wiri Sandra'

Leptospermum 'Princess Anne'

- 'Blossom': (D), 2 m, winter and spring to summer, green foliage
- 'Cherry Brandy': (S), 75 cm, spring, new growth bronze purple
- 'Gaiety Girl': (D), 1.5 m, spring, reddish foliage
- 'Kea': (S), 30 x 45 cm, autumn to early winter, compact habit, olive-bronze foliage, flowers hidden
- 'Keatleyi': (S), 2–3 m, winter and spring, large pink flowers flushed with white
- 'Martinii': (S), 2–3 m, late winter to spring, white flowers flushed with crimson
- 'Rosy Morn': (D), 1.5 m, autumn to spring, compact habit
- 'Sunraysia': (D), 2 m, pink flowers fading to white
- 'Tui': (S), 1.5 m, spring, white flushed with crimson, erect habit
- 'Wiri Sandra': (S), 1.3 m, spring, pink, upright habit

REDS
- 'Crimson Glory': (D), 1 m, spring, reddish brown foliage
- 'Huia': (S), 30 x 45 cm, spring, compact habit
- 'Kiwi': (S), 30–90 cm, spring and early summer
- 'Red Damask': (D), 2 m, late winter to mid-summer, compact, bronze foliage
- 'Red Ensign': (S), 2 m, winter and spring, bushy upright habit
- 'Winter Cheer': (D), 1.5 m, winter to early spring, bushy habit, reddish foliage
- 'Wiri Amy': (S), 1 m, winter to spring, conical habit
- 'Wiri Donna': (S), 1.5 m, spring, flowers with yellow stamens, vigorous
- 'Wiri Kerry': (D), 80 cm, autumn through to spring

Manuka cultivars at Auckland Regional Botanic Gardens

- Herb 40–50 cm high
- Full sun to semi-shade
- Tolerant of dry conditions
- Intolerant of wet conditions
- Wind hardy
- Frost hardy
- OK in coastal gardens

THE DIFFERENCES BETWEEN
MANUKA AND KANUKA

HEIGHT: kanuka is generally the taller of the two.
BARK: the bark of an adult manuka flakes off in much coarser strips than kanuka.
LEAVES: kanuka leaves are very soft, while manuka's are quite needle-like to the touch. Kanuka leaves are often bright green in colour, while manuka is darker.
FLOWERS: manuka flowers are two to three times bigger than kanuka and occur singly, where kanuka tends to occur in small clusters.
SEED CAPSULES: manuka capsules are four to five times bigger than those of kanuka and stay on the plant all year round. Kanuka capsules open only a few months after flowering and then fall to the ground.

The heart-shaped leaves of the kawakawa are 5–10 cm in diameter and a flat dark green to almost yellow-green colour, depending on the amount of sunlight the plant is getting and the richness of the soil. The young red branches zigzag, straightening a little as they get older, and eventually the kawakawa will attain a height of 2–3 m. Although it is not fast growing it bushes well with little or no pruning. The flowering spikes, up to 8 cm in length, are not showy and occur on separate male and female plants. The fleshy fruiting spike that forms on the female plant turns a yellow to orange colour on maturity; although not outstandingly showy, these fruit do provide food for the birds.

Kawakawa foliage

Kawakawa is found throughout the North Island and down to Banks Peninsula and Okarito in the South. It occurs naturally in lowland forest.

LIKES AND DISLIKES: Although kawakawa seems to prefer moist rich soils, in cultivation it often does better in a free-draining soil, especially in humid areas of the far north. In such areas kawakawa is very prone to fungal attack, primarily black spot, so it is best to plant it in drier, more free-draining conditions that are exposed to at least some air movement. In full sun the leaves of kawakawa will be thicker and a more yellow-green colour; the growth rate will also be a little slower. Conversely, in the shade the leaves will be darker green and thinner. Kawakawa will grow in either place quite happily; it just depends on the look you prefer. Like many coastal species kawakawa will only tolerate light frosts.

PESTS AND PROBLEMS: Leaf-chewing insects are a naturally occurring problem that the kawakawa has been dealing with for thousands of years. They will not kill the plant, but you can spray with a systemic insecticide if the holey leaves worry you. Black spot is a more serious problem which can be lethal, although it is amazing how little can appear to be left of a kawakawa and yet it will very slowly come back to life. At the first sign of blackening on the stems or leaves, spray with a fungicide. When the plant is very young it can also be prone to slug and snail attack on the new leaves. Planting your kawakawa in the right position to start with will minimise all these problems.

CARE AND MAINTENANCE: You can prune your kawakawa to shape it, but remember that the buds appear to occur half-way up the petiole and that more than two shoots can form at each node. If the plant is showing signs of discoloration in the shade, feed it or preferably compost and mulch it, ensuring as always that the compost is well matured.

When propagating kawakawa from seed you can easily end up with a thicket in your propagation tray. To avoid this, break the fruiting spike down with sharp propagation sand, squashing it with your fingers, or use a pestle and mortar on the fruit then mix the ensuing paste with the sand. *TIP TIME: Coarse propagation sand is good to use for fruit with a number of seeds in them, or for fruit that are individually tightly packed. The sand not only helps separate the seed from the fruit but also acts as a thinner, reducing the number of seeds in a handful and allowing it to be sprinkled over the tray more evenly.* If using seed,

A compact bush of *Macropiper melchior* with young nikaus in the foreground

remember to slug bait the tray. Cuttings can also be taken with reasonable success.

LANDSCAPING SUGGESTIONS: Kawakawa is a bold green bushy plant that is ideal for shady conditions. If the ground is a little damp, ensure that the root run of the plant will be cool and preferably that there is some air movement. Kawakawa is one of the few native species that form a dense bush in the shade and have large leaves, consequently it is ideal for planting under older established plantings that have started to open out below the canopy. The foliage can look excellent against some of the smaller-leaved divaricating coprosmas and with *Myrsine divaricata*, *Astelia banksii* and forest cabbage tree. In a dry, shaded corridor between two buildings it could be planted with tree ferns, *Hebe diosmifolia*, *Astelia banksii*, ground ferns and grasses, or it could be grown as a pot plant in a shaded part of a deck or courtyard.

SIMILAR SPECIES: *Macropiper excelsum* subsp. *peltatum* (syn. *M. excelsum* var. *majus* and *M. excelsum* forma *psittacorum*) has glossier leaves than *M. excelsum* and they are more yellow green in colour even when in the shade. The young branches are of a similar colour, not the red of *M. excelsum*. The leaves also tend to be slightly larger.

Macropiper melchior, the most striking of the three forms mentioned here, occurs only on the Three Kings Islands. The leaves are very lush and glossy, dark green and undulating. The disadvantage of this spectacular plant is that it is the most temperamental. It is very, very prone to black spot and

- Shrub 2–3 m tall, 1–2 m wide
- Semi-shade to shade
- Dry or free-draining soil
- Wind tolerant
- Tolerant of very light frosts
- OK in coastal gardens

Phytophthora. The ideal spots for it are in very free draining soil, under well-established vegetation or under a large eave of a roof where very little rain penetrates. Air movement and light shade are both beneficial. Do not under any circumstances put an automatic irrigation system on it; water only if necessary. *M. melchior* is very frost tender and not very tolerant of cold winters.

Muehlenbeckia astonii

The fine, dark, zigzagging branches of *Muehlenbeckia astonii* interlace with one another to form a dense, almost tidy, ball of branches up to 3 m round. On these branches are very small heart-shaped leaves, only a few millimetres across, that almost seem suspended in the bush. After rain or heavy dew, when the bush is laden with small droplets of water that glisten in the sunlight, you will realise why you planted this species. In cooler parts of the country *Muehlenbeckia astonii* is completely deciduous; elsewhere this depends on the winter temperatures. The delicate white flowers form in summer and are followed by translucent white fruit with a small black seed suspended inside.

Muehlenbeckia astonii is found only at Palliser Bay in the North Island and on the eastern side of the South Island to Banks Peninsula. It occurs on the coast and on lowlands, especially terraced riverbeds.

A bush of young *Muehlenbeckia astonii* with kiokio underneath

LIKES AND DISLIKES: Its main dislike is excess moisture, which will often lead to root rot, although if the plant has a cool root run this is not a problem. It prefers dry conditions, and seems to thrive in them. It is tolerant of light shade, and exposure has little effect. A very hardy species for dry areas.

PESTS AND PROBLEMS: *Muehlenbeckia astonii* is one of those wonderful species that is pest and problem free.

CARE AND MAINTENANCE: Since it prefers dry conditions, it pays to keep irrigation away from *Muehlenbeckia astonii*. Compost and mulch will provide food for the plant, but make sure the trunk is left clear. If the soil is very rich initially, *Muehlenbeckia astonii* may grow upwards at the expense of developing secondary tissue. *FACT TIME: The new growth of shoots is called primary growth, and is often green and very soft. Over time secondary thickening will develop which has supporting tissue in it that will make the branch sturdier. If a plant is growing too vigorously, it will often put more energy into primary, shoot, growth at the expense of secondary, supporting, growth. If this is the case, the young plant may require staking to keep it upright. Often the stake will not need to be tied* on to the plant, but can be threaded through the branches into the ground below. *Muehlenbeckia astonii* can easily be pruned to shape, and will respond quite quickly.

Propagation is by cuttings or seed, depending on what is available.

LANDSCAPING
SUGGESTIONS:
The unusual form of *Muehlenbeckia astonii* makes it a wonderful contrast plant. For example it can look quite striking planted in front of *Griselinia*, whau or kawakawa, or in a coastal planting with *Astelia* species, hebes, *Coprosma repens*, rengarenga and *Pimelea prostrata*. For a stark alpine or grassland look, it could be planted with mountain totara, *Chionochloa, Carmichaelia arenaria, Carex* species and *Scleranthus*. *Muehlenbeckia astonii* is ideal as a hedge in dry, exposed conditions where it can be planted as a uniform species or mixed with a species like *Olearia lineata*; silver and black, subtle but elegant. It is good to plant *Muehlenbeckia astonii* where its delicate beauty can be seen, so the 'droplet' changes can be appreciated — the leaves, the flowers, the fruit and of course the water.

The fine interlacing branches and small heart-shaped leaves of *Muehlenbeckia astonii*

- Shrub 2–3 m round
- Full sun to semi-shade
- Dry hardy
- Wind hardy
- Frost hardy
- OK in coastal gardens

Ngaio is a very hardy species that is very fast growing in exposed situations. Its only real disadvantage is that it is poisonous to stock, so it should not be planted anywhere near where stock graze or can reach. It forms a large, compact shrub in exposed conditions, or a small tree 5 m or so in height in sheltered conditions that are more conducive to growth. The leaves are what could be termed 'classic' in terms of shape — wider in the middle and tapering to either end. They are generally pale olive green in colour, although in the Nelson area a form has been found that is almost bright green. This form is becoming very popular in cultivation. Ngaio can be very wide spreading in its habit, but it can be pruned and will respond very

Adult ngaio

quickly. The small white flowers have delicate purple spots on them and are followed by small reddish purple fruit.

Ngaio occurs from the far north to south Otago, generally on the coast or in coastal forests.

LIKES AND DISLIKES: Very wet soils and very shady sites do not bring out the best in ngaio and should be avoided if possible. Apart from this, it has no strong likes or dislikes and is tolerant of poor soils. As a juvenile, ngaio can be frost tender.

PESTS AND PROBLEMS: Ngaio is basically pest and problem free, an indication of its hardiness.

CARE AND MAINTENANCE: Apart from a prune to keep it to the desired height or shape, all ngaio will require is a good mulch or compost once a year to help keep up plant vigour.

Remember to keep the trunk of the tree clear.

Cuttings are the most common means of propagation and they take quite readily. Strangely though, the cuttings take, or root, over a long period; in one batch of cuttings some will start to root after 3 weeks and some will take 2 months. Applying bottom heat will reduce the variation in rooting time.

LANDSCAPING SUGGESTIONS: Ngaio is an ideal plant to use in exposed conditions, whether coastal or otherwise. The lovely rounded habit of a mature tree can look quite spectacular silhouetted against the skyline, either in a group or as a single specimen. If you use ngaio as a hedge line, you will find that as they mature the base of the trees will become quite clear. This space can be underplanted with species such as flax, rengarenga lilies and hebes. Its fast growth rate also makes ngaio an ideal species to use as a nurse crop, providing protection and shelter for other larger, more slow-growing species such as *Nestegis montana*, totara, kowhai and rata.

CULTIVARS AND VARIETIES:
• *Myoporum laetum* 'Purpureum' is a purple-leaved form of ngaio, slower growing and a little shorter in habit.
• *Myoporum laetum* var. *decumbens* has larger leaves that are more leathery and is more prostrate in its habit, reaching about 2 m in height. A mature plant is dense and slightly sprawling but can look quite wonderful; it is an underutilised species, especially in exposed situations, even if it is more frost tender.

- Large shrub up to 6 m tall
- Up to 4 m wide
- Full sun to semi-shade
- Dry tolerant
- Wind hardy
- Frost tender as a juvenile
- Coastally hardy

Myoporum laetum var. *decumbens*

Mapou averages 3–4 m in height so it will suit all but the smallest of gardens. Its habit is an attractive pyramidal shape, often with a clear trunk at the base. The branches and petioles are a lovely dark red when young, providing a base for smallish, wavy-margined leaves that are green mottled with red and sometimes yellow. The small flowers are insignificant, as are the small black fruit, although they do provide food for birds.

Mapou occurs throughout New Zealand on forest margins and in scrubland from sea level to montane forests.

LIKES AND DISLIKES: Mapou will tolerate most situations. In quite shady situations it will become stretched and if it is very wet, *Phytophthora* can become a problem, but these are really the only concerns. In poor soils mapou will tend to be more yellow, but it will still slowly grow. The ideal growing conditions are a rich, free-draining soil in full sun, not too exposed.

PESTS AND PROBLEMS: As long as very damp sites are avoided there are no major pests or problems.

CARE AND MAINTENANCE: Strangely, if mapou is planted into soil that is too rich, it can outgrow itself, especially in the early stages. Its growth will tend to be very soft, and it will be unable to support itself. If this happens, stake the plant and do not feed it until it has strengthened and can support itself. Mapou can be pruned to shape but will take a little time to recover.

Seed is the most common form of propagation, though cuttings can be taken.

LANDSCAPING SUGGESTIONS: Mapou can be used as a hedging species if it is pruned to shape from an early age, and its narrow habit makes it ideal along a driveway or similar confined space. The disadvantage is that its growth rate is only average. Its classic habit means that it could be grown as a small specimen tree underplanted with *Myrsine divaricata, Asplenium oblongifolium, Heliohebe* and grasses. It can also be planted on the margin of a larger border, its shape and coloration providing a point of interest.

CULTIVARS: *Myrsine australis* 'McKenzie's Gold' has variegated leaves that are yellow down the midrib and the primary veins. It is a good foliage plant for floral work.

> • Small tree 3–4 m in
>   height
> • Full sun to semi-shade
> • Wind tolerant
> • Dry tolerant
> • Tolerant of poor soils

Mapou foliage and red branchlets

Myrsine australis 'McKenzie's Gold'

Weeping mapou specimen

Cascading branchlets of weeping mapou

Weeping mapou is one of the more attractive of New Zealand's divaricating plants. As the name suggests, the stiff interwoven branches curve downward to create a cascading effect. These branches can range in colour from grey to pink, even to pale orange. The leaves are very small and heart-shaped, and like the flowers are of little significance. The form of the plant is its main feature. It is very slow growing but will eventually reach a height of about 2 m in cultivation.

Myrsine divaricata is found throughout the country from Kaitaia south. It tends to occur in localised populations from sea level to 1220 m, in scrubland and lowland to higher montane forests.

LIKES AND DISLIKES: *Myrsine divaricata* is intolerant of wet situations, especially in warm, humid areas. Conversely, it is very tolerant of dry conditions, surviving where many species would fall by the wayside. In full sun it forms a stocky, densely divaricating bush, while in the shade it becomes just a little stretched, the degree of stretching being dependent on the degree of shading.

PESTS AND PROBLEMS: Weeping mapou is one of those delightful species that is pest and problem free.

CARE AND MAINTENANCE: A thick layer of mulch will improve plant vigour, but remember to keep the mulch well away from the trunk. For a tighter plant, do not overfeed.

Propagation is by both cuttings and seed. Cuttings take some time to establish because of the 'woodiness' of the species.

LANDSCAPING SUGGESTIONS: Weeping mapou's tolerance of a range of light levels can be used to create an interesting effect, with a planting going from full sun through to shade. Keep the foreground planting low, and remember that weeping mapou is slow growing and that you do not want to hide its characteristic form. As the plants grow taller others could be added, starting in full sun with *Acaena inermis* 'Purpurea' as a groundcover, *Festuca coxii* and *Podocarpus nivalis*, moving into parahebes, small flax cultivars, grasses and *Muehlenbeckia axillaris,* and finishing with *Asplenium oblongifolium,* rengarenga, Chatham Island forget-me-not and *Fuchsia procumbens* as a groundcover. Bold species like *Meryta sinclairii* and *Griselinia lucida* help to accentuate the form of *Myrsine divaricata*, but it can also look quite outstanding as a specimen in a bed of grasses. It could be planted in a pot with *Scleranthus* at its base, or *Blechnum pennamarina.*

- Shrub approx. 2 m tall
- Full sun to shade
- Prefers dry, free-draining conditions
- Wind hardy
- Frost tolerant
- OK in coastal gardens

This species differs from *Olearia albida* in that it has much thicker leaves, with leaf margins that are tightly undulating, like corrugated iron. The leaves are 4–6 cm long x 2–3 cm wide. They are a pale grey-green colour and when crushed have a delicate lemon fragrance; if you have a good sense of smell, this is apparent as you brush past the plant. The flower heads that form in summer are made up of clusters of small white daisy-like flowers that form a small white 'umbrella'. As a shrub, *Olearia albida* var. *angulata* has a much tighter habit than *O. albida* but is slower to gain height, although it does bush well. It is much hardier in warmer parts of New Zealand, being less prone to *Phytophthora*. It can reach a height of 2–3 m.

It occurs on the coast of the North Island from North Cape to Reef Point.

LIKES AND DISLIKES: *Olearia albida* var. *angulata* requires free-draining or dry soil conditions; avoid planting it in damp areas at all costs. While it prefers full sun it will tolerate some shade, tending to lose its naturally very bushy habit. Wind exposure is not a problem.

Olearia albida var. *angulata* bushes to ground level

PESTS AND PROBLEMS: In damp conditions *Olearia albida* var. *angulata* can suffer from root rot; if this occurs the leaves will become yellow and a young plant will become very unstable in the ground. The best thing to do is to prune the plant back quite hard, lift it and plant it somewhere that is a lot drier; spraying with a systemic fungicide will speed recovery. Lemon tree borer can be a problem; it should be pruned out and/or the plant sprayed with a systemic insecticide. If the plant is very stressed it can become susceptible to rust, which can be dealt with by spraying with a mixture of lime sulphur and colloidal sulphur. If it is affected with *Olearia* gall midge, spray with summer oil and a contact insecticide, and where possible remove the galls.

CARE AND MAINTENANCE:
In full sun and free-draining soil *Olearia albida* var. *angulata* will require little maintenance. It can be pruned to shape and will respond moderately quickly. When mulching and composting remember to keep well away from the trunk, as it is susceptible to collar rot.

Cuttings are the preferred method of propagation, and most species of *Olearia* root moderately readily. Seed can also be used, but the young seedlings can be very susceptible to fungal attack.

Foliage of *Olearia albida* var. *angulata* showing its strongly corrugated margins

LANDSCAPING SUGGESTIONS: Its grey/green coloration and quite stiff leaves make this an interesting contrast plant to use in the garden. Its slow growth rate makes it less desirable as a hedging species, but the foliage is a wonderful addition to a mixed planting, especially if conditions are harsh. Plant it with *Corokia cotoneaster*, *Hebe macrocarpa*, mapou and *Pseudopanax laetus*, or on the coast as a specimen shrub surrounded by Chatham Island forget-me-not, *Muehlenbeckia astonii*, *Hebe speciosa* and small-leaved *Coprosma* groundcovers. It can also be used as a border plant to a back drop of rata, *Griselinia lucida*, lancewood and kanuka.

- Shrub 2–3 m tall
- Full sun to semi-shade
- Dry tolerant
- Wet intolerant
- Wind hardy
- Frost hardy
- OK in coastal gardens

Olearia lineata is one of the hardiest of the *Olearia* species, but it is not well known in the north. It has very fine silver-green leaves that are 2–4 cm long by only a few millimetres wide. When it is young, it is difficult to see how an adult plant can be anything but the wispiest of specimens. As the shrub establishes, however, it continues branching, creating a specimen that has a delicacy that few other plants can match. On maturity it attains a height of 2–3 m, and the flowers, although small, are quite fragrant. A selected form of *Olearia lineata*, *O. lineata* 'Dartonii', is most commonly grown in cultivation and referred to simply as *Olearia lineata*. It is very fast growing and the leaves are slightly longer and more silvery. The discussion deals with this form.

Olearia lineata is found from north Westland and north Canterbury southwards, in lowland to lower montane forests and forest margins, and on river terraces.

LIKES AND DISLIKES: Although it occurs naturally only in the South Island, *Olearia lineata* is very tolerant of humid conditions, unlike most *Olearia* species. It is also quite happy in exposed situations, even coastal winds. It prefers full sun but is entirely tolerant of light shade.

PESTS AND PROBLEMS: *Olearia lineata* is not as susceptible to disease as many olearias; see *Olearia albida* var. *angulata* for problems that may arise if the plant is very stressed.

CARE AND MAINTENANCE: *Olearia lineata* requires little maintenance. In good growing conditions it pays to prune once or twice a year to keep a tight habit; if you prefer an open, weeping habit, prune as necessary. It responds very quickly to pruning, especially if pruned during a growing season. The amount of composting and mulching you do depends on the growth rate you require, as *Olearia lineata* is tolerant of very poor soils.

LANDSCAPING SUGGESTIONS: *Olearia lineata* is ideal for hedging: it does not create a solid boundary, it is very fast growing, tolerant of very exposed conditions, and responds well to pruning. *TIP TIME: A good hedge should not block the wind, it should break its flow. If the hedge creates a solid wall, the wind will hit it, rise up over the top and dump its full force on the other side. Where it falls will depend on the height of the hedge. A slightly open hedge, which the wind can penetrate, will not eliminate airflow on the sheltered side but will greatly reduce its force.* Olearia lineata can just as easily be planted as a specimen tree; you can let it grow naturally, with the branches weeping and bushing to ground level, or train it into a single-leader plant for the first metre or so then allow the lax branchlets to cascade around it. Glossy-leaved plants like *Heliohebe, Myosotidium, Asplenium* and in warmer areas *Xeronema* will all look good against it. *Acaena inermis* 'Purpurea' and *Muehlenbeckia axillaris* also work well as groundcovers. As always *Chionochloa flavicans* and other native grasses could be used; in the wind the whole planting would be mobile!

- Shrub 2–3 m tall
- Full sun to semi-shade
- Wind hardy
- Frost hardy
- Tolerant of poor soils
- Coastally hardy

Fine grey-green foliage of *Olearia lineata*

A well-clipped hedge of *Olearia paniculata*

Olearia paniculata foliage

This is a very common hedge species in the South Island, but in the warmer north it can be prone to root rot, so is not as common in cultivation. It is a large shrub that forms a dense bush 2–4 m in height, and if planted in the open can become a small spreading tree at least 3 m wide. The leaves are very distinctive, with lightly undulating margins and yellow-green colour on the upper surface. Like most olearias, the underside of the leaves has a fine tomentum, in this case white to buff coloured. The leaves are lightly scented when crushed, but any smell they have is overshadowed by the intense fragrance of the small, inconspicuous flowers that form in autumn, which can permeate the air for many metres around the plant.

Olearia paniculata occurs through both islands from Raglan to Greymouth on the west coast and from East Cape to Oamaru on the east coast. It can be found in lowland to lower montane shrubland and on forest margins.

LIKES AND DISLIKES: See *Olearia albida* var. *angulata*.

PESTS AND PROBLEMS: See *Olearia albida* var. *angulata*.

CARE AND MAINTENANCE: In warmer areas, if planted in rich soil, *Olearia paniculata* can outgrow itself and may need to be staked upright until the new growth has hardened. If this is a problem, it is advisable not to overfeed the plant; the result will be a tighter, hardier shrub.

LANDSCAPING SUGGESTIONS: *Olearia paniculata* can be pruned into a hedge with great success. I have seen a very interesting hedge that had been developed out of old plants. The inner side of the hedge had been pruned back entirely to expose the wonderfully gnarled main trunks, while the outside had been left untouched. The effect was that of an old tree-fuchsia forest, or 'goblin forest'. The coloration of *Olearia paniculata* makes it ideal for planting with species like *Olearia lineata*, *Hoheria sexstylosa*, lancewood and cabbage trees. If planted as a specimen tree, small-growing manuka cultivars, *Muehlenbeckia astonii*, *Brachyglottis* and grasses could be planted around it.

- Large shrub 2–4 m tall, 2–3 m wide
- Full sun to semi-shade
- Dry tolerant
- Wet intolerant
- Wind hardy
- Frost hardy
- OK in coastal gardens

Karo has a number of good features: it is relatively fast growing, tolerates coastal winds, tolerates quite dry conditions, and naturally has a moderately dense habit. The leaves are dark green and leathery, approximately 5 cm x 2 cm, with a fine grey tomentum underneath; they are not dissimilar to pohutukawa and very like feijoa, with which karo can be confused. The new growth is almost completely covered in tomentum and appears completely grey. *FACT TIME: Species with tomentosed leaves (i.e. covered in fine hairs) are nearly always suitable for planting into a coastal garden. The fine hairs act as a protection against the harsh coastal winds, helping prevent moisture loss and salt damage. Species with thick glossy leaves are also generally suitable.* Karo can grow to 6 m or more in sheltered areas; in very exposed regions it may only reach 3 m. With the arrival of spring comes the formation of small (1 cm) fragrant deep red flowers that eventually become black seed capsules.

Karo foliage and deep red flowers

Karo is found naturally from North Cape to Poverty Bay, on streamsides, forest margins and along the coast.

LIKES AND DISLIKES: If karo is grown in soil that can become waterlogged it will tend to lose its leaves. This will not kill the plant, unless the conditions are severe, but it will knock it back. It is better to plant it in drier, more free-draining conditions. If planted in the shade, karo will stretch to try and find light, while in full sun it will have a more compact habit. While it seems to thrive in coastal conditions, faster growth can be attained by providing a windbreak for the first two to three years. The plant will extend above the windbreak as it establishes.

PESTS AND PROBLEMS: Karo is a remarkably tolerant plant and fairly problem free. It is susceptible to psyllids, but the effect on the plant is minimal. It can be treated with a systemic insecticide, but this is only necessary for cosmetic purposes.

CARE AND MAINTENANCE: It is advisable to prune at least once a year (in northern areas) if you want to keep the height of the tree down or maintain a specific shape. It is also advisable to prune back to a leaf node (the point where the leaf attaches to the stem) that sits on the upper surface of the branch, rather than the lower. Equally, karo can be left to its own devices to grow into a small tree or a large shrub. To achieve optimal growth and plant health it is advisable to compost and mulch regularly, avoiding contact with the trunk of the tree. Granular or foliar feeds can be used, but they do not improve soil structure and their effects are often quite short-lived.

Seed is by far the easiest means of propagation. Cuttings can be taken but they take a while to root because of the woody nature of the species; a heat bed is advisable.

LANDSCAPING SUGGESTIONS: Karo's tolerance to exposed conditions makes it ideal as a hedging species, either on its own or mixed with species like *Pseudopanax laetus*, purple akeake and whau. Being slightly smaller, karo is more suited to smaller inner city gardens than kohuhu and tarata, and requires less maintenance if a smaller plant is required. In some situations karo will form a clear trunk. If this is not the desired form, rather than pruning heavily to try and force budding lower down, try underplanting. By doing this you not only achieve your aim of filling the empty space but you also create a three-dimensional effect with structure. In a sunny position plant *Phormium* cultivars, *Brachyglottis greyi* and native grasses, and in semi-shade *Asplenium oblongifolium*, *Hebe diosmifolia* and *Libertia*.

- Large shrub
  3–5 m tall
- Full sun to semi-shade
- Dry tolerant
- Wind hardy
- Frost tolerant
- OK for coastal gardens

P*ittosporum eugenioides* is not really a shrub as it can grow to over 8 m in height, but for convenience it is described with the rest of the genus. Its common name, lemonwood, arises from the fragrant lemon scent the leaves release when crushed. If planted in full sun, tarata will bush to ground level, unlike some other species of *Pittosporum*. The large leaves can grow as long as 15 cm, although they are usually about 10 cm. They are elliptical to oblong in form (about 2 cm wide) with wavy margins, and are a pale glossy green. The bark is very pale and can become a feature in itself if the tree is pruned to capitalise on it. Tarata is often used as a hedging plant, as it is very hardy and grows quickly, but it can be also used as a feature tree. Its tapering juvenile habit fills out to a large bushy tree as an adult. As with many

Pyramidal form of young tarata

A mixed planting of *Pittosporum* cultivars

native species the small pale cream flowers are insignificant, but they do have a delicate lemon fragrance that is most noticeable on still, warm days.

Tarata is one of New Zealand's most widespread pittosporums, being found throughout the country from lowland to mountain forests of around 600 m.

Variegated tarata

LIKES AND DISLIKES: Unlike most species of *Pittosporum,* tarata will tolerate heavier soils — but note, the word is tolerate. The better the growing conditions, the better the growth rate. It will tolerate moderately windy sites, but not to the same extent as karo, and if planted in a shady site tarata will become more open in its habit.

PESTS AND PROBLEMS: The leaf spotting that can occur on tarata is entirely natural and seems to be more common as the temperatures cool through autumn and winter. The new growth in spring tends to come through quite clean. See *Pittosporum crassifolium* for further information.

CARE AND MAINTENANCE: See *Pittosporum crassifolium.*

LANDSCAPING SUGGESTIONS: The fast growth rate and hardiness of tarata make it ideal for hedging, although it is better suited to less exposed sites. Try planting a mixture of species rather than just the one; in a windy site try mixing it with pukanui, karo, *Olearia lineata* and even cabbage trees, which provide a different form. In sheltered areas tree ferns could be added to provide yet another form. A border or hedge does not necessarily have to be bushy to the ground. Once the trees start to form clear trunks, other lower-growing species can be added and before you know it you have what could be termed a natural boundary.

CULTIVARS:
• *Pittosporum eugenioides* 'Variegatum' is a variegated form of tarata with irregular cream to pale green margins. The foliage is commonly used in floral arrangements. Its growth rate is slower than the true species, as is the case with most variegated plants.
• *Pittosporum eugenioides* 'Variegatum Minimum' is not only a smaller-growing form but also has smaller foliage and a tighter habit.

- Tree 5–10 m tall, 3 m wide
- Full sun to semi-shade
- Tolerant of damp soils
- Moderately wind hardy
- Frost hardy

Like tarata, kohuhu is very fast growing and very hardy. It will tolerate drier and colder conditions, but not wetter. Like karo, it will tend to drop its leaves if it gets too wet, but this will not kill it unless the conditions are extreme. Kohuhu grows to a height of 4–6 m and a width of 2–3 m. The leaves are very variable in size and shape, from small delicate leaves of only 1 cm to large leaves of 5 cm or more. This variability is largely regional. Kohuhu has its tightest habit in full sun and can form a tight ball if the conditions are right. These conditions are normally cooler and drier than the norm — harsh but not too harsh! In warm, humid areas with long growing seasons kohuhu can grow too vigorously and may require more pruning to keep a dense habit.

Pittosporum 'Irene Paterson'

Pittosporum 'Deborah'

Like tarata, kohuhu is found throughout New Zealand in coastal and lower montane forests. In the South Island it tends to be restricted to the drier eastern side of the alps.

LIKES AND DISLIKES: See *Pittosporum crassifolium*, but note that kohuhu is not tolerant of coastal conditions.

PESTS AND PROBLEMS: Aphids can cause malformation of new shoots, which can be dealt with by spraying with an insecticide; a systemic insecticide will give longer benefit. See *Pittosporum crassifolium* for further information.

CARE AND MAINTENANCE: See *Pittosporum crassifolium*.

LANDSCAPING SUGGESTIONS: Kohuhu and many of its cultivars are ideal for hedging, but remember that the variegated species will tend to be slower growing. Try planting kohuhu with *Griselinia lucida, Hoheria sexstylosa* and *Olearia lineata*; the latter will add softness to the planting. Kohuhu will usually form a clear-based tree but this can be underplanted once the gap is large enough to plant into. If the space is sunny, *Astelia banksii* could be planted with native grasses and irises. If semi-shady, plant *Adiantum hispidulum* and rengarenga lilies, using *Fuchsia procumbens* as a groundcover.

Pittosporum 'Tom Thumb'

CULTIVARS:
• *Pittosporum* 'Argenteum Variegatum' has blackish stems with small light grey-green leaves with creamy margins. It grows to 3–4 m.
• *P.* 'Deborah' has leaves that are greyish green with cream margins and flushed with pink; 2 m.
• *P.* 'Goldstar' has gold and green leaves with a cream midrib; 1.5 m.
• *P.* 'Irene Paterson' has leaves that are almost white flecked with green when new. As the leaves age they become more green. It is an excellent species for contrast. Very slow growing (2–3 m).
• *P.* 'James Stirling' has small pale green leaves on blackish branchlets; 3 m.
• *P.* 'Limelight' has leaves that are dark green with bright lime green variegations; 3–5 m.
• *P.* 'Mountain Green' has an excellent habit. It has small bright green leaves and grows to 2–5 m.
• *P.* 'Pixie' is a small compact shrub that grows to 1.2 m. It has small grey-green leaves.
• *P.* 'Silver Magic' has small pale green leaves with a silver margin which contrast with the fine black branches; 3 m.
• *P.* 'Silver Sheen' has pale silvery green leaves and fine black branches; 3 m.
• *P.* 'Sunburst' has rounded to oval, green, yellow and cream variegated leaves. The leaves become lime green on maturity, when it can reach 2 m.
• *P.* 'Tandarra Gold' has golden variegations; 3–4 m tall.
• *P.* 'Tom Thumb' is very slow growing and reaches only 75 cm. The young growth tends to be green, changing to a deep red then purple on maturity.
• *P.* 'Variegatum' differs from the other silver variegated species in having a larger, flatter, more pointed leaf; 4–6 m.

• Small tree 4–6 m high, 2–3 m wide
• Full sun to semi-shade
• Dry tolerant
• Frost hardy
• Intolerant of coastal conditions

P*seudopanax laetus* is a large-leaved species that can provide a wonderful dark green backdrop to a sizeable garden bed, if you have the space. It forms a large shrub that can be 3–4 m in diameter, but its size and shape can be controlled with regular pruning. Although it can be slow to gain height in full sun it bushes well as it grows. The dark glossy green leaves are made up of 5–7 oval leaflets that combine to form a palmate leaf, just like its close relative *Pseudopanax arboreus*. The middle leaflet is the largest and can be 25 cm or more in length. The leaves are borne on attractive long dark red petioles; the same colour can sometimes be found on the margins of the leaflets. If designing a garden with birds in mind then consider this species, or any other *Pseudopanax*. Although the flowers, borne on separate male and female plants, are very small and of little interest to the birds, they are attracted to the large groups of small berries that are commonly borne on female plants in spring.

This species of *Pseudopanax* is found only in the North Island and only from the Coromandel Peninsula to Taranaki.

LIKES AND DISLIKES: Although a lot hardier than *Pseudopanax arboreus* in damp conditions, especially in the more humid north, *Pseudopanax laetus* is a little susceptible to root rot. If you are planting it into ground that can become very wet, try planting densely around the base of

Bold green foliage of *Pseudopanax laetus*

the plant to provide a cooler root run. Conversely, it is tolerant of dry conditions. Unlike many species, *Pseudopanax laetus* still bushes well in light shade. In very harsh, windy conditions the margins of the leaves can become burnt and a little unsightly. In these conditions, consider planting *Pseudopanax lessonii* instead.

PESTS AND PROBLEMS: *Pseudopanax laetus* can develop distorted leaves if it becomes stressed. However, if you alleviate the stress the new leaves will be normal.

CARE AND MAINTENANCE: When pruning this species cut back to a leaf node, remembering that a new branch will form from the axil of the leaf you have pruned to, so that is the direction the branch will go. If the leaf faces the outside of the shrub, the branch will go to the outside, and if the leaf faces into the middle of the bush the new branch will grow into the middle. *Pseudopanax laetus* buds very easily from the leaf axils and responds well to even very severe prunings, although it can take time to recover. As with any large shrub, regular composting or mulching will greatly improve plant vigour.

Pseudopanax arboreus

Seed is by far the easiest means of propagation, although cuttings can be used if that is the only material available.

LANDSCAPING SUGGESTIONS: It is best to plant *Pseudopanax laetus* where it can slowly grow and spread to its full glory, hence eliminating the need to prune. Its dense glossy green habit makes it an ideal backdrop for more unusual species like *Coprosma virescens*, *Carmichaelia arenaria* and *Corokia* species. It is also effective as part of a large mixed planting with kowhai, northern rata, *Nestegis montana* and lancewood.

SIMILAR SPECIES: *Pseudopanax arboreus* can grow to twice the height of *P. laetus* and is not as tolerant of wet conditions, especially in humid areas; it will tolerate damp conditions in cooler southern areas. *P. arboreus* occurs naturally along the coastline, often mixed with other shrubby species like mahoe and *Coprosma*.

- Large shrub 3–4 m tall, 3 m wide
- Full sun to shade
- Dry tolerant
- Wind tolerant
- Frost hardy

It can be difficult to find hardy shrubs for exposed coastal conditions, but houpara is one of them. It can grow to 3–4 m x 1–2 m, and in exposed situations has a very solid habit. The very leathery leaves are palmate, like many of the *Pseudopanax* species, but they are not large; the central oval leaflet only reaches about 10 cm in length. The berries of the houpara provide excellent bird food in summer. This species of *Pseudopanax* readily hybridises with *P. crassifolius* (lancewood), and if a batch of hybridised seed is sown the resultant seedlings will show a huge variation from almost pure houpara to almost pure lancewood. This variation has led to many different cultivars.

Houpara occurs naturally only in the North Island as far south as Poverty Bay.

LIKES AND DISLIKES: Houpara is not tolerant of damp soil conditions, preferring dry or free-draining soil. For a bushy plant, position it in full sun and, if growth rate is not too important, an exposed place. Coastal conditions are not a problem, the only effect being a slower growth rate.

PESTS AND PROBLEMS: Houpara is generally pest free and the only problem is wet soils.

CARE AND MAINTENANCE: See *Pseudopanax laetus*.

LANDSCAPING SUGGESTIONS: Houpara is ideal for coastal gardens and can be planted as a specimen bush amongst a low planting, for example with *Coprosma acerosa*, *Pachystegia insignis*, *Sophora* 'Dragon's Gold', *Hebe* species and *Carex testacea*. It can also be used as a wind break, allowing less wind-hardy species to be planted behind it. In a city garden it can be used as a backdrop for other species, such as *Muehlenbeckia astonii*, *Corokia* and even smaller-growing cultivars of manuka.

CULTIVARS:
• *Pseudopanax* 'Adiantiformis' has a leaf shaped rather like that of a duck's webbed foot. It likes similar conditions to *P. lessonii*, but its habit tends to be more erect. It is probably a selected hybrid of *P. lessonii* and *P. crassifolius*.
• *Pseudopanax* 'Cyril Watson' differs from houpara in that the leaflets are fused together to form a single leaf. This is a very popular cultivar that is often used for container planting.
• *Pseudopanax lessonii* 'Gold Splash' is very similar to houpara but has yellow variegations splashed along the veins and midribs of the leaves.
• *Pseudopanax lessonii* 'Nigra' is a bronze-purple leafed form of houpara. The winter leaves have the strongest colour, as the plant is not growing. In spring and early autumn the new leaves can be quite green with only a purple margin. *P. lessonii* 'Purpureus' and *P. lessonii* 'Nigra' are virtually identical but have marginally different leaf colours.

• *Pseudopanax* 'Linearifolius' is again very probably a hybrid of *P. crassifolius* and *P. lessonii*. The leathery leaves usually have 3–5 leaflets and can be quite linear in form; they may become 3-foliate or even singular as an adult. *P.* 'Linearifolius' grows to 2–3 m, is quite erect in its form, and will tolerate dry shady conditions.

• *Pseudopanax* 'Trident' is similar to *P.* 'Adiantiformis' but can have two forms of juvenile leaves, 3-pronged or single. The single leaves become more prominent as the plant matures. It has a very upright habit.

• Large shrub 3–4 m tall, 1–2 m wide
• Full sun to semi-shade
• Dry hardy
• Wet intolerant
• Wind hardy
• Tolerates light frosts
• Coastally hardy

Top: *Pseudopanax* 'Cyril Watson'

Middle: *P. lessonii* 'Gold Splash'

Bottom: *P.* 'Trident'

The common name for horopito is very apt as the leaves have the highest concentration of 'pepper' of any plant in the southern hemisphere. It is a very attractive plant and one that is easy to grow. In a garden situation it will grow to around 2 m, but very slowly. It has a narrow habit, as can be deduced by the angle of the branches. *Tip time: If you are unsure what shape a shrub will have, look at the angle of the branches. If they are upright and close to the centre of the plant, the habit will tend to be contained; if the branches are more perpendicular to the trunk or branch from which they have come, the plant will tend to be more wide spreading.* The sturdy branches are almost black in colour and contrast with the often multi-coloured leaves. The upper surface of the leaves can vary in colour from a uniform light olive green to a mottled green that is dotted with red and has red margins. The best red colorations occur in full sun. The undersides of the leaves are white to glaucous. The flowers are relatively insig-nificant, as are the small dark fruit.

Flowers and fruit of horopito

Horopito occurs naturally throughout both main islands except in the very north of the North Island. It is found in lowland to higher montane forest and can form thickets after forest destruction.

LIKES AND DISLIKES: Horopito will tolerate full sun through to quite deep shade. Exposure is not a problem, and it will grow quite happily in a range of soil moistures, from dry to moderately damp, although it is not happy in very dry or very wet conditions. Horopito is very hardy.

PESTS AND PROBLEMS: There are no common pests or major problems.

CARE AND MAINTENANCE: Horopito requires minimal maintenance. It will require pruning very rarely, if at all, and mulching can be done with the rest of the garden, avoiding the trunk of the tree.

Seed is the more common means of propagation although cuttings can be taken, and are essential for propagating a plant that has particularly good leaf coloration.

Speckled multi-coloured foliage of horopito

LANDSCAPING SUGGESTIONS: Horopito is an ideal species for even the smallest of gardens, although its very slow growth rate makes it difficult to use as a specimen. Try planting a group of horopito with *Myrsine divaricata*, *Metrosideros perforata*, *Astelia banksii*, *Parahebe* species and *Muehlenbeckia axillaris*. Alternatively put it in the foreground of a large mixed planting, with *Meryta sinclairii*, *Olearia albida* var. *angulata*, *Pseudopanax* species, *Hoheria sexstylosa* and northern rata. Horopito can also be grown in a pot and put by the kitchen door for times when the cook is feeling adventurous enough to make use of its peppery leaves; *Blechnum pennamarina* could be used as a groundcover underneath it.

- Shrub 2 m tall
- Full sun to shade
- Dry tolerant
- Wet tolerant
- Wind tolerant
- Frost hardy

Like all vines, the native *Clematis* species prefer to have a cool root run. In the wild, vines tend to germinate in the shade then meander up into the canopy, where the light levels are higher, before flowering. New Zealand's *Clematis* are all evergreen, so they can easily be distinguished from the exotics, which are deciduous. *C. paniculata* is by far the most popular species as it has the largest, whitest flowers. The male plant has flowers that are 5–10 cm in diameter, larger than those of the female, but the female has the added attraction of the soft, downy seedheads that form after flowering. The juvenile leaves consist of a number of leaflets that tend to stabilise at three in the adult plant. The leaves can vary greatly in shape.

Male flowers of *Clematis paniculata*

Clematis paniculata occurs naturally throughout New Zealand, commonly in lowland and lower montane forests.

LIKES AND DISLIKES: To avoid potential problems plant *Clematis* in a free-draining, shaded site that has some air movement.

PESTS AND PROBLEMS: *Clematis* can be difficult to grow, especially in humid areas. If the ground is too wet it can be susceptible to *Phytophthora*; if it is too humid downy mildew can be a problem, and then there is always rust, which can be treated with copper oxychloride. As a juvenile, *Clematis* can also be prone to snail and slug damage.

CARE AND MAINTENANCE: In humid areas it is advisable to keep a wary eye on your *Clematis* and nip any problems in the bud, so to speak. A thick layer of mulch every year will help keep the soil cool and improve its structure, as well as providing nutrients.

Propagation can be by cutting, but to ensure you get the right sex they must be taken after flowering. If the sex does not matter seed can be sown, but be careful as you may end up with thousands of young *Clematis*! Don't over-water the seed tray, and slug bait it.

LANDSCAPING SUGGESTIONS: Many people plant *Clematis* at the base of a trellis or pole, which is perfectly fine, but how about planting it on the southern side of an established tree and letting it grow into the crown of the tree, then watch it flower. Unlike some of the exotics, native *Clematis* species are not vigorous enough to smother trees. The main thing to remember when planting *Clematis* is that it likes to have shaded roots. If you don't have a suitable site, plant thickly around the base of the plant or use large rocks, which will absorb most of the heat. Once a *Clematis* is established most of its foliage will be in the upper reaches where there is more light, so in some senses it takes up very little room in a garden, and it can look quite spectacular in the spring.

Clematis foetida in full flower

SIMILAR SPECIES: *Clematis cunninghamii* has smaller foliage and flowers than *C. paniculata* (male flowers are 2–3 cm in diameter) but the pale green flowers tend to form in large clusters and have a delicate honey scent.

Clematis foetida also has smaller flowers (male flowers 2.5 cm in diameter) which are a pale green colour but they have quite a strong, sweet fragrance.

Clematis forsteri has leaves of a similar size to *C. paniculata* but again has honey-scented flowers that are pale green. The male flowers are 3–4 cm in diameter.

- Vine
- Semi-shade to shade
- Dry, free-draining conditions
- Wind tolerant as an adult
- Frost hardy

The climbing rata is another species that has separate juvenile and adult habits. A young climbing rata either starts on the ground, normally in a shaded environment, or as an epiphyte perched on a tree. If it starts life in the open, it will transform into an adult plant. Like any vine, the first thing the young plant does is start growing towards the light above. Rata do not have tendrils as such, but they do have numerous fine roots that form on the stems, and sometimes even on the leaves. These roots attach themselves to the tree on which they are climbing and carry the plant upwards. The leaves of a juvenile rata normally lie in one plane so the stem is as close as possible to the tree it is climbing. The very tall vine that can eventually form develops a very stout stem. Once the plant reaches the light, which may be many metres above, it slowly changes into its adult form. This does not climb but forms a bush, and the leaves do not lie in one plane but form a whorl. Once the vine has transformed into an adult it will then flower. The moral of this story is, when purchasing a climbing rata remember to ask for a juvenile plant if you want a climber and an adult plant if you want a bush! They can change from one to the other but because of their very slow growth rate this will take time.

Carmine rata has small dark green leaves and as an adult has small (2–3 cm) pohutu-kawa-like flowers that smother the plant in spring. The bush that is formed grows to about a metre in height and width, but slowly.

Carmine rata occurs naturally only in the northern half of the North Island, as far south as East Cape and Taranaki. It tends to occur in coastal forest, forest margins and scrubland.

Carmine rata flowers

Carmine rata climbing against a wall

LIKES AND DISLIKES: All climbing rata prefer a free-draining soil. Plant it in the sun if you want a bush and the shade if you want a vine. The adult plant especially is very tolerant of windy conditions, and in such situations forms a very tight bush. Carmine rata is frost tender.

PESTS AND PROBLEMS: Climbing rata are virtually pest and problem free, not even being susceptible to the psyllid that can ravage pohutukawa.

CARE AND MAINTENANCE: The branches of adult climbing rata tend to be very brittle so be careful when working around them. However, if they do break the plant fills in the space fairly quickly, especially once the plant is established. Although carmine rata can tolerate poor soils, the plant will be more lush if fed regularly.

Metrosideros perforata

Cuttings take readily and are the preferred means of propagation. Remember, if you want a climber take from a juvenile plant, and for a bush take from an adult.

LANDSCAPING SUGGESTIONS: Carmine rata is ideal for any garden with dry or free-draining soil and will tolerate very harsh conditions. If planting it as a vine, remember that it is very, very slow, sometimes climbing only 10–20 cm in a year. The bush can also take time to establish but is worth the wait. The small glossy leaves look excellent with divaricating plants like *Muehlenbeckia astonii* and *Corokia cotoneaster*, and with the grey of *Pachystegia* or *Astelia banksii*. It can be used as a small shrub to go around the base of kowhai or even wheki, if it is planted in full sun. If an adult climbing rata is planted on the margin of a shaded area, the new growth on the shaded side can revert to its juvenile form and will creep along the ground or up tree trunks.

SIMILAR SPECIES: *Metrosideros diffusa* has small oblong leaves that can have a lovely orangey hue to their new growth. Unlike many of the climbing rata, *M. diffusa* will form an attractive sprawling bush on the ground, even as a juvenile plant. The flowers are generally not as profuse as on *M. carminea* and tend to be white with a pink flush.

Metrosideros fulgens is the most slow growing of the species mentioned here. It has larger leaves that are shaped more like those of tree rata, and larger flowers that are coloured apricot through to red.

Metrosideros perforata is very similar to *M. carminea* but has small white flowers in summer and is frost tolerant. It is also slightly faster growing. The new growth can shoot out from the main bush, creating a very sculptural effect. It is becoming a lot more readily available.

- Vine or bush of 1 m
- Full sun or shade
- Wind hardy
- Dry tolerant
- Tolerates coastal conditions

Parsonsia heterophylla • KAIHUA, NATIVE JASMINE

This is a vigorous vine which is very variable in its leaf size and shape, and has a distinct juvenile form. The juvenile leaves, which are sometimes almost brown, tend to be narrower. As the vine ages the leaf colour changes to dark green above and pale below. The leaf shape can still be entirely variable on a mature plant and even from plant to plant—a nice characteristic for those of us who abhor consistency! To support itself in the open the fine branches will often wind around themselves, creating a 'rope' on which the plant can gain some height. The small fragrant white to yellow flowers are up to 10 mm long and are borne on a flowering spike up to 10 cm long. Flowering normally occurs in spring, followed by the formation of long seed pods that can be quite attractive.

Native jasmine occurs throughout New Zealand from coastal to lower montane forests (900 m).

LIKES AND DISLIKES: Native jasmine requires a cool, shaded root run and preferably something to climb up so that it can reach the sunlight, where it will flower. It prefers a free-draining soil and will tolerate very dry conditions. It is intolerant of wet conditions, particularly in humid areas.

PESTS AND PROBLEMS: There are no major pests and problems.

CARE AND MAINTENANCE: The vine can easily be cut back if necessary. Mulch will keep the ground moist and provide nutrients; ensure that it is kept well away from the main stems.

LANDSCAPING SUGGESTIONS: Native jasmine is a vigorous climber that can be used to cover a trellis, or it can be planted at the base of a tree and allowed to climb to the top where its flowers will be seen to good effect. On the coast or in other large open areas it could be left to sprawl over the ground, climbing over itself and any contours that you or the land provide; it can be kept contained by being mown or trimmed with a weed-eater once or twice a year. Remember to keep the roots cool then just leave it to grow.

SIMILAR SPECIES: *Parsonsia capsularis* is very similar but has less leaf variation; a single plant tends to have a single leaf form. The fragrant flowers and the spikes are usually smaller. The flower colour varies from white to yellow to dark red, although the more strongly coloured form *P. capsularis* var. *rosea* is not widely available.

- Prefers its roots in the shade
- Dry tolerant
- Wet intolerant in humid areas
- Wind tolerant
- Frost hardy
- OK in coastal gardens

Parsonsia heterophylla
in full flower

Tecomanthe speciosa flowers

Tecomanthe speciosa

This species is one of today's conservation success stories; at one time there was only one plant left in the wild, on the Three Kings Islands. The large glossy green leaves are made up of 3–5 leaflets; the central leaflets are the largest and can grow to 13 cm long x 6–7 cm wide. It is quite tropical looking for a native plant. If planted in the right conditions *Tecomanthe* can grow quite rampantly. The flowers are like those of the kowhai in shape, but occur in larger clusters and are up to 3 cm long. They are a pale cream-green colour, and in texture not unlike a waxy *Rhododendron*. The flowers appear in autumn and sometimes again in winter, and tend to hang within the foliage. *Tecomanthe* does not have tendrils, but instead has branches that instinctively wind themselves around whatever is available. If there are no other tree branches, it will wind around itself.

The only place that *Tecomanthe* occurs naturally is on the Three Kings Islands.

LIKES AND DISLIKES: If conditions are too good, the *Tecomanthe* vine seems to keep growing and growing and growing but not flowering! Wind seems to have a minimal effect on its growth rate and appears to encourage earlier flowering. There are three environmental conditions that should be avoided—wet feet, full sun and frost. If you don't have a shady site, try planting other plants around the base of the vine, or place large rocks around it; either method will create a cool root run for the vine. If the site is too wet, the plant will quickly show signs of stress, normally through leaf loss and a yellowing of the leaves. *Tecomanthe* is very frost tender.

PESTS AND PROBLEMS: If the plant is showing stress from conditions that are too wet, move it promptly, or lift it and plant it on a mound. It is then advantageous to spray the plant with a fungicide, which will speed its recovery. Apart from this, *Tecomanthe* is virtually problem and pest free.

CARE AND MAINTENANCE: *Tecomanthe* will tolerate any form of pruning, i.e. there are no special techniques. Food will improve its growth, whether it be mulch, compost, liquid feed or granules. If the plant is hungry, the leaves will turn a more yellow green.

LANDSCAPING SUGGESTIONS: *Tecomanthe* has more roles in the garden than most native vines. With its very rapid rate of growth it can be used as a hedging plant, although it will need some support, which can easily be created with a few posts and two or three wires. As *Tecomanthe* is very hardy coastally it is an ideal species to plant as a windbreak, and after establishment less hardy species can be planted behind it. In the right conditions *Tecomanthe* can cover at least a metre of wall, or fence line, in a year. The flowers naturally hang in among the leaves and the best way to enjoy them is often from inside the house when the vine grows over or past a window. If *Tecomanthe* is planted in the shade, it will head for the light like any other vine and will only flower once it gets there.

- Prefers its roots in the shade
- Dry tolerant
- Wet intolerant
- Wind hardy
- Very frost tender
- Coastally hardy

In the north and other relatively frost-free areas rengarenga is used extensively in amenity plantings such as on traffic islands and in parks. It can tolerate full sun and quite deep shade, and is virtually unaffected in exposed windy sites. The soft grey-green strap-like leaves can grow to over 50 cm long, while the overall width of the plant can reach 80 cm or more. The width of the leaves varies considerably, depending on where the plant was originally sourced. The wider-leaved form, from Matapouri Bay in the far north, is the one most often grown in cultivation. It is also a little more glaucous in colour and is believed to be slightly more resistant to snail attack, a major problem with rengarenga. Although the foliage is attractive, the flowers of the rengarenga are the *piéce de résistance*. The large erect panicles extend well above the foliage in spring, with the abundant, often pink, buds opening to form small white flowers. The buds tend to open first at the base of the panicle, moving through to the tip, a process that can take 3–4 weeks.

Flower spike of rengarenga

Rengarenga occurs naturally throughout the North Island and on the northern tip of the South Island. It is more common on the coast but can be found on rocky exposed cliffs inland and even beside waterfalls within the forest.

LIKES AND DISLIKES: The leaves of rengarenga will burn in even a light frost, but this will cause no lasting damage to the plant. If the frost is severe enough to burn off all the leaves, don't panic straight away, you might find that in the spring it will regrow from the growing tips at ground level. Rengarenga can look stunning in a semi-shaded situation, where it tends to stand very erect, its light grey foliage contrasting with the often dark backdrop. If planted where there are high winds, it will tend to be shorter and tighter in habit. Rengarenga is tolerant of very dry sites but less so of wet.

PESTS AND PROBLEMS: Snails and slugs love rengarenga and will happily munch their way through a plant if left to their own devices. To avoid this, plant the rengarenga in a dry or free-draining environment, spray with insecticide, or go on nightly hunting missions until the pests are under control.

CARE AND MAINTENANCE: If you prefer a tidy-looking plant, the old leaves can be pulled out easily. If the leaves of a healthy plant start to yellow and/or become shorter, it will probably benefit from feeding (you can use liquid or granular food, or compost).

Rengarenga can be propagated by seed or by division. When dividing it, cut the foliage back to reduce the stress on the plant, and keep it damp but not wet. *TIP TIME: When dividing a plant remember to hold the two parts you are separating as low down as possible and pull gently. As the plant starts to separate move your hands further down, into the space you have created, and again pull gently. Continue doing this until the two pieces are completely separated, right down to the end of the roots. If the plant is very large you may need to use a spade to do the initial separation. Remove any damaged segments as they will probably die off and may provide an open wound for fungus to penetrate.*

A border planting of rengarenga

LANDSCAPING SUGGESTIONS: Where you put rengarenga depends on how vigilant you are about snail baiting! If you are vigilant, you can plant it anywhere as long as it is not too wet. Otherwise avoid anywhere damp or moist, especially in full sun. In the shade rengarenga can look especially effective when planted with ferns like *Asplenium oblongifolium* and hen and chicken fern. On the coast it can be planted with flaxes, astelias, puka and cabbage trees, and in a cottage garden with *Linum*, *Parahebe*, *Hibiscus* and *Hebe*. Its simple form allows it to meld into any existing planting, but remember that it can get quite large. Its rapid growth rate also makes it an excellent plant to use in a new garden as it quickly provides some substance.

CULTIVARS:
• *Arthropodium* 'Matapouri Bay' has a wider leaf than most other forms.
• *Arthropodium* 'Parnell' also has a wide leaves.

> • 50–60 cm tall, 80 cm wide
> • Full sun to shade
> • Prefers free-draining or dry conditions
> • Wind tolerant
> • Frost tender
> • OK coastally

Astelias range from the large *Astelia grandis* and *A. chathamica* to the smaller forms of *A. nervosa* and *A. graminea*, and some even smaller species that are not commonly in cultivation. The two most common grey astelias are *A. chathamica*, with its broad strap-like leaves, and *A. banksii*. *Astelia banksii* is smaller and more delicate than *A. chathamica* and has finer leaves. It is slower to gain height but bulks out readily, a process known as 'pupping'. If it is planted in a shady position, *Astelia banksii* will gain height more quickly and pup more slowly: for height, plant in the shade; for bulk, plant in the sun. The leaves are generally about 3–4 cm wide x 1 m long, although they can grow to 2 m or more in time. Astelias have separate male and female plants. The fruit, found only on the female, is small and white, often flushed with magenta. The fruit are tightly packed on a flowering stalk of 30 cm or more.

Astelia banksii

Astelia banksii is found in the northern half of the North Island, generally coastally on exposed rocky cliffs or in lowland forests.

LIKES AND DISLIKES: *Astelia banksii* prefers a dry, free-draining soil and will perch on rocky cliffs, reliant on the little rainwater that it can catch. It tolerates full sun and somewhat shady conditions, and is also tolerant of coastal conditions. A hardy species!

PESTS AND PROBLEMS: *Astelia banksii* is intolerant of wet or even moist conditions, where it becomes very susceptible to *Phytophthora*. This is lethal if not caught early enough, so if you notice the tips of the leaves and the centre of the plant starting to discolour, move the plant and spray it with a systemic fungicide. Early frosts can be a problem for plants with a lot of fresh new growth. There are no significant pest problems.

CARE AND MAINTENANCE: *Astelia banksii* requires no real maintenance. The old leaves can be pulled off but this is

Astelia chathamica

not necessary.

Although the seed of astelias can take a year or more to germinate this is the easiest way to obtain a large number of plants. *Astelia banksii* also withstands division.

LANDSCAPING
SUGGESTIONS:

Astelias have texture, colour and form and there is one for most situations. *Astelia banksii* is an ideal pot plant, particularly for those of us who

Coloured astelias

forget to water our plants. It can be planted on its own, with a groundcover or with small grasses like *Festuca coxii*. This can add colour as an underplanting, but remember that it is slow and that the grey colour becomes more of a blue green in the shade. Native grasses look good with *Astelia banksii* and are easy to remove and transplant once the astelia starts to establish; allow space for the grass to grow to its full width without crowding the astelia. *Heliohebe hulkeana*, Chatham Island forget-me-not and *Pachystegia* all look good planted with *Astelia banksii*, whether it be in a rock garden or on the coast.

SIMILAR SPECIES: *Astelia chathamica* has leaves up to 10 cm wide x 2 m long. The clump tends to stand at around 1.5 m, with the erect leaves falling over quite acutely rather than weeping like *A. banksii*. It is a very dominating plant because of its stoutness and grey coloration. It is frost hardy but intolerant of high moisture. *Astelia* 'Silver Spear' is a selected form.

Astelia fragrans averages about 1 m in height, although the olive-green leaves can be up to 2 m long. Although the leaves are quite wide, the plant has a graceful weeping habit like *A. banksii*. This species is intolerant of wet conditions in the north of the North Island.

Astelia grandis is a very similar olive green to *A. fragrans* but more erect in its habit and tolerates wet swampy ground throughout New Zealand. It will tolerate growing in water and is also tolerant of reasonably dry conditions. Its habit is very similar to that of *A. chathamica*.

Astelia nervosa has leaves that vary from a grey green to a red grey. It usually grows to around 50 cm, although it can reach 1 m or more. It is intolerant of high humidity and/or high moisture in the Auckland area northwards; it is better not to plant it in this area unless you have a suitably dry spot, like under the eave of a roof.

Astelia solandri has foliage of a lovely spring green colour which can become red on the tips if planted in full sun. It is very similar to *A. banksii* in habit and size, and likes the same conditions. In the wild it can be seen as an epiphyte.

- 1–1.5 m tall and wide
- Sun to shade
- Requires dry conditions
- Wet intolerant
- Wind hardy
- Frost tolerant
- Coastally hardy

Although commonly referred to as a grass, *Carex* is actually a native sedge. As a genus it occurs throughout New Zealand. *C. trifida* can be found in very wet situations, *C. buchananii* in very dry; *C. testacea* is found on the coast, while *C. dissita* is found in the forest. They are diverse in colour and size, and in general very hardy as long as you find the right *Carex* for the conditions. Use the table below to help you choose.

PESTS AND PROBLEMS: There are no major pests or problems.

CARE AND MAINTENANCE: *Carex* require little maintenance and even less care. The long seedheads may need to be pulled out of some species as they can flatten the plant, while in others the old leaves should be pulled out to allow the new shoots to develop and to prevent 'matting'. In some cases the plant may benefit from being reduced in size, with half the tussock being cut off, which again allows new leaves to develop.

Propagation is by seed or division; both are equally successful.

Grasses make ideal container plants

LANDSCAPING SUGGESTIONS: Grasses can be used to underplant existing vegetation, either on their own or with other species like the divaricating weeping mapou and *Coprosma rhamnoides*, or the glossy green *Asplenium oblongifolium* or kawakawa. They look very effective on an exposed bank where the wind can swirl through them, and in an open situation they provide a contrast to the leaves of flowering plants. They can be used as a border plant in front of a larger planting, and the larger

Carex comans 'Frosted Curls'

grasses can be used as a low hedge to mark off different areas of the garden. They also work well in planters, sitting up above the ground with the long leaves trailing over the pots; if placed in a windy position, the leaves move even better than on the ground. *Carex buchananii* is ideal for this.

Carex testacea with hebes

Species	Colour	Leaf width (mm)	Height (cm)	Wet	Dry	Wind	Sun	Semi-shade	Shade
Carex 'raotest'	Green	Rolled	45	N	Y	Y	Y	Y	N
Carex albula	Straw to pale green	Rolled	45	N	Y	Y	Y	Y	N
Carex buchananii	Red brown	Rolled	75	N	Y	Y	Y	Y	N
Carex comans 'Bronze'	Tawny brown		30–40	N*	Y	Y	Y	Y	N
Carex comans 'Frosted curls'	Light green	Rolled	N*	Y	Y	Y	Y	Y	N
Carex comans 'Green'	Apple green								
Carex dipsacea	Green	Rolled	75	N*	Y	Y	Y	Y	N
Carex dissita	Bright green	6–7	45–80	N*	Y	X	Y	Y	Y
Carex flagellifera 'Bronze'	Bronze	3–5	35–75	N*	Y	Y	Y	Y	N
Carex flagellifera 'Green'	Green	3–5	35–75	N*	Y	Y	Y	Y	N
Carex geminata	Green	7–10	50–100	Y	N	Y	Y	Y	N
Carex lessoniana	Green	7–10	50–100	Y	N	Y	Y	Y	N
Carex secta	Green	3–5	100	Y	Y	Y	Y	Y	N
Carex tenuiculmis	Bronze	2–4	75–100	Y	Y	Y	Y	Y	N
Carex testacea	Green, orange tips	3–5	50–60	N	Y	Y	Y	Y	N
Carex trifida	Blue/green	8–12	60–90	Y	Y	Y	Y	Y	N
Carex virgata	Dark green	2–5	100	Y	Y	Y	Y	Y	N

KEY: Y = yes; N = no; * = will tolerate wetter conditions in cooler areas or where they can have a cool root run.

Although *Chionochloa flavicans* is often referred to as a miniature toetoe, the species are not closely related. The leaves are approximately 10 mm wide and up to 1 m long, and they arch over to form the classic tussock grass form. The mid-green leaves have a faint blue hue to them, especially if the plant is growing vigorously. The main feature of this plant, though, is its beautiful flowering plumes, 50 or more. These begin forming in late spring and last for many months; in fact, the old plumes can remain on the plant until the following season. The flowerheads are not unlike those of toetoe in form — long and silky, with a weeping habit. They are pale green when young, going through to a creamy white as they age. They stand well above the foliage and can be up to 1.5 m long.

The different species of *Chionochloa* tend to be very localised in their distribution. *C. flavicans* is restricted to the east coast of the North Island in localised areas from Coromandel to Hawke's Bay. It tends to occur on rocky outcrops and cliff faces from sea level to about 970 m.

LIKES AND DISLIKES: In warm humid areas *Chionochloa flavicans* is very susceptible to *Phytophthora* so it needs to be planted in a spot that is either very dry or very free draining. It will tolerate full sun and semi-shade equally well, and exposed conditions are preferable, minimising disease problems. In cooler areas or where it has a cool root run, it will tolerate moist soil conditions.

Chionochloa flavicans showing the multitude of flowering heads

PESTS AND PROBLEMS: As long as the moisture levels in the soil are not allowed to creep up there are no major pests or other problems.

CARE AND MAINTENANCE: If the plant is being attacked by fungus, the foliage will begin to brown off and the leaves will become more yellow green in colour. At this point it is better to dig it up and move it to a drier spot, as *Phytophthora* is likely to continue to be a problem. A diseased plant will come out of the ground very easily, as it will have very few healthy white roots. The amount of foliage you will need to cut off will depend on the number of healthy roots; the fewer roots the more foliage you will need to remove. When replanting, remember not to bury the base of the leaves. If you don't want to move the plant, cut it well back and spray it with a systemic fungicide. Ideally, lift it and replant it on top of the ground.

Propagation can be by seed or division. Fungus can kill a small plant very quickly, so make sure your potting medium has very good drainage and the humidity is not too high. Do not over-water!

LANDSCAPING SUGGESTIONS: A fully grown plant can be over a metre in diameter if given the room to spread, a point to remember if planting a large swathe. You can vary the look you create by varying the spacing between the plants: for an undulating effect, plant a metre apart; for an even top height, plant around 50–60 cm apart. The classic tussock form and tidy habit of *Chionochloa flavicans* mean it can stand on its own as a specimen and also meld in with other plants in a mixed planting. It could dominate a small rockery with species such as *Heliohebe*, *Parahebe* 'Snowcap', *Acaena inermis* 'Purpurea' and *Pimelea prostrata*, or it could be planted underneath an open tree like kowhai where the light levels are still quite high. The tips of the leaves can become a little burnt off in very exposed sites but it is still worth planting there; it could be planted with *Astelia*, flaxes, kowhai and whau. *Chionochloa flavicans* can also come into its own on the sunnier sides of well-established large trees or hedges, especially where the larger trees sap most of the moisture out of the ground.

SIMILAR SPECIES: *Chionochloa flavescens* is very similar to *C. flavicans* but has a very open flowerhead.

Chionochloa rubra (red tussock) has tawny bronze leaves that appear quite slender, as they are rolled like a fine tube. It grows to 1–1.5 m in height and again has a fine open flowerhead that extends above the tussock.

> - Tussock grass up to 1 m tall
> - Full sun to semi-shade
> - Dry hardy
> - Wet intolerant
> - Wind hardy
> - Frost hardy
> - OK in coastal gardens

Although grass-like in its form, turutu is a member of the lily family. It has soft olive-green leaves that are 10–15 mm wide, while the plant itself averages 60 cm in height. Turutu can form very stout underground rhizomes that can spread 10 cm or more from the parent plant. Over many years the plant can become quite wide-spreading, the centre of the plant dying out to leave a clear space in the middle, like an atoll with a reef of foliage. In summer the very small flowers, carried on flowering spikes that extend well above the 'tussock', transform into relatively large berries. These vary in colour from white flushed with lavender through to deep purple, and hang on the spike like small jewels, hence the common name 'blue-berry'. This is another underutilised species that is easy to grow and maintenance free!

It occurs throughout New Zealand on open dry hillsides through to shady forest floors.

LIKES AND DISLIKES: Turutu prefers dry, free-draining conditions but does not mind whether it is planted in sun or shade. If the site is very exposed, the tips of the leaves may become burnt.

PESTS AND PROBLEMS: Root rot can become a problem if conditions are too moist.

CARE AND MAINTENANCE: The old leaves can be pulled off if a clean and tidy look is required. The plant can be propagated by division, but do not break it down into pieces that are too small.

LANDSCAPING SUGGESTIONS: Turutu is excellent as a low filler, and ideal for dry spots under existing vegetation, where it could be planted with kawakawa, *Coprosma rhamnoides*, *Astelia banksii* and *Carex dissita*. In a low mixed planting *Parahebe*, Marlborough rock daisy, *Linum*, *Sophora* 'Dragon's Gold', *Muehlenbeckia astonii* and turutu could be planted together. It is effective planted en masse with *Corokia cotoneaster* as the emergent species, planted individually or in small groups.

CULTIVARS: *Dianella nigra* 'Variegata' is a variegated form that is white and pale green. It is an excellent contrast plant in the shade.

> - Herb 60 cm tall
> - Full sun to shade
> - Dry tolerant
> - Wet intolerant in warm areas
> - Wind tolerant
> - Frost hardy

'Tussock' of turutu

The often deep purple berries of turutu

The native *Euphorbia* is not as floriferous as many of the exotic species. The flowers are very small but are surrounded by tiny deep purple 'leaves' (actually bracts) that contrast with the silvery blue of the foliage. The flowers nestle in among the uppermost leaves and can be quite hard to see. *Euphorbia* is a very hardy species but is moderately vigorous and ideal for filling a dry empty space. The often non-branching stems can grow up to a metre high, and if allowed the plant can be many metres wide. The underground runners that form are very strong and penetrate even very compacted soil; they can spread up to 50 cm from the plant in one hit!

Euphorbia is considered rare and endangered in the wild, and is found only in a few localised coastal areas.

LIKES AND DISLIKES: *Euphorbia* requires a free-draining soil but will tolerate full sun through to light shade. Wind exposure is not a problem, even coastally.

PESTS AND PROBLEMS: The only major pest or problem is rabbits, which consider *Euphorbia* to have been planted just for them. They will decimate it!

CARE AND MAINTENANCE: As this is such a vigorous species it will require cutting back to maintain it in a confined space. The new shoots are easily hoed, reducing the spread. When it is cut back the stems do not resprout; resprouting occurs from the base of the plant.

Seeds or cuttings can be used for propagating. When taking cuttings soak them in a bucket of cold water until the white sap stops oozing from the cut face; this improves the cutting take.

LANDSCAPING SUGGESTIONS: *Euphorbia* is ideal in a large coastal garden, where it could be planted with cabbage trees, whau, karaka, manuka and grasses. If it is planted with taller-growing species, *Euphorbia* can be left to grow where it wants to; after a few years other species can be planted in any gaps that are left. *Euphorbia* is also excellent in a suburban garden but will have to be weeded out from among adjoining species in a mixed planting; it can easily be cut off at ground level and if well shaded, will not readily resprout. To minimise maintenance *Euphorbia* could be planted in a large well-drained container dug into the ground, pre-determining and containing its spread. With its lovely blue-grey foliage and stems, *Euphorbia* provides a contrast in virtually any planting. It is particularly effective with *Pseudopanax*, *Sophora* 'Dragon's Gold', *Corokia cotoneaster*, flaxes and *Muehlenbeckia axillaris*.

- Herb up to 1 m tall
- Full sun to semi-shade
- Dry tolerant
- Wet intolerant
- Wind hardy
- Tolerates light frosts
- Coastally hardy

Euphorbia glauca

Festuca coxii

Festuca is a true grass genus. *Festuca coxii* is often confused with *F. glauca*, an Australian grass that has a much tighter, smaller-growing habit. *F. coxii* has a lovely fine rolled blue-green leaf. It stands 20–40 cm tall, depending on conditions, and forms a loose open tussock. The very open flowerheads extend above the foliage and are a pale tawny blue colour.

Its distribution in the wild is confined to the Chatham Islands.

LIKES AND DISLIKES: *Festuca coxii* requires a dry, free-draining soil and prefers high light levels. Exposure is not a problem, coastally or elsewhere, and it is completely frost hardy.

PESTS AND PROBLEMS: *Phytophthora* can be a problem if the soil is too wet. If this occurs, dig up the plant, cut back the foliage, and transfer it to a drier site. The plant will usually recover completely without your having to spray with a systemic fungicide.

CARE AND MAINTENANCE: The tussock can be 'combed' with the fingers occasionally to pull out the old leaves. Sometimes *Festuca* can become very stretched and lose its classic tussock shape. If this happens, dig the plant up, cut back the foliage and replant it in the same spot, but bury the tawny base of the leaves. The tussock will return to its former glory in no time at all. *Festuca coxii* can be propagated by division, or seed can be sown.

LANDSCAPING SUGGESTIONS: *Festuca coxii* has a softness and colour that make it a wonderful addition to any garden, whether cottage, rockery or tropical. In addition to providing a contrast to other plants it can look equally good on its own, perhaps in a courtyard or stony pathway, or in a pot. In a rockery it looks effective with *Heliohebe hulkeana*, *Myosotidium*, *Carmichaelia arenaria* and *Xeronema*. In a cottage garden, *Linum*, *Geranium traversii*, *Parahebe* species and rengarenga may be planted with it. A bed of *Festuca coxii* could also be planted around the base of *Tecomanthe* to help keep the soil cool when it is planted in the sun, while on the coast a large bed could be planted with groups of *Xeronema* and the occasional *Corokia cotoneaster*.

SIMILAR SPECIES: *Festuca actae* is very similar to *F. coxii* but has a slightly more upright habit and a taller, more erect flowering spike. It likes the same conditions as *F. coxii* and keeps its blue-green colour best when divided once every couple of years.

- Grass 30–40 cm high
- Full sun to semi-shade
- Requires dry conditions
- Wind hardy
- Frost hardy
- Coastally hardy

Of the few species of native geranium, *G. traversii* is by far the most floriferous. It is a low-growing perennial herb, ideal for exposed situations and for well-tended city gardens. It can withstand very dry situations, since it has a taproot that not only provides water during droughts but also 'taps' deep-seated water sources. *FACT TIME: This feature is not uncommon in herbaceous plants that occur naturally in very dry environments, whether in gravelly terrain or desert conditions.*

Geranium traversii has deeply dissected grey-green leaves that are covered in fine hairs on both sides and are about 40 mm in diameter. The leaves all join in the middle of the plant, forming an attractive flat rosette that extends to a short flowering spike in late spring and through summer. The flowers are about 2.5 cm in diameter and are normally white to pink. Runners can form from the main plant and will form their own rosettes and even root into the ground, hence slowly spreading like a groundcover. This species has been used to help create a number of very successful *Geranium* hybrids overseas.

Geranium traversii occurs naturally only on coastal cliffs on the Chatham Islands.

LIKES AND DISLIKES: *Geranium traversii* prefers dry conditions; its main dislikes are moisture and high humidity. It will grow happily in full sun or light shade, and exposure is not a problem.

PESTS AND PROBLEMS: Fungal attack can occur if moisture levels are too high, especially when combined with high humidity.

The pink and white flowers of *Geranium traversii*

CARE AND MAINTENANCE:

To prevent the plant seeding prune off the dead flower-heads, which will also help maintain plant vigour and encourage even more flowering. If the plant is becoming too widespread, some of the runners can be pruned back; if they have rooted into the ground, they will need to be dug up.

Geranium traversii can be propagated from seeds or by transplanting rooted-off shoots. Seeds will obviously produce much greater numbers.

Bronze foliage and pink flowers of *Geranium* 'Pink Spice'

LANDSCAPING SUGGESTIONS: *Geranium traversii* can be used in a rockery, and is ideal for border planting among other low-growing plants like *Podocarpus nivalis*, Chatham Island forget-me-not and native grasses. On the coast it could again be planted with Chatham Island forget-me-not and smaller-growing flax cultivars, Poor Knights lily (in warmer areas), hebes and astelias. As long as it does not become too shaded by other species *Geranium traversii* will slowly wander through a planting, following the light.

CULTIVARS:
• *Geranium traversii* 'Elegans' is a selected form that has bright pink flowers with darker veins.
• *Geranium* 'Pink Spice' has lovely bronze foliage and bright pink flowers, which tend to be smaller than those of *G. traversii*.

> • Very low-growing herb
> • Full sun to semi-shade
> • Prefers dry or free
>   draining soil
> • Wind hardy
> • Frost hardy
> • OK in coastal gardens

Heliohebe hulkeana, syn. *Hebe hulkeana* • NEW ZEALAND LILAC

Heliohebe hulkeana stands out from other hebe-like species with its very dark glossy green foliage and very long upright light purple flower spikes. (These are often erroneously described as blue; in fact very few New Zealand native plants have a true blue colour.) It flowers from late spring through to summer. This species can look stunning, particularly when planted in a harsh sunny exposed site. In the right situation it can form an attractive shrub of approximately 50 cm tall.

The northeastern part of the South Island is the natural home of this species — an area renowned for its low humidity and moderately low rainfall, something to remember when finding a spot for it in the garden.

LIKES AND DISLIKES: *Heliohebe hulkeana* is very susceptible to downy mildew in regions of high humidity; in such areas plant it in a spot exposed to the prevailing winds. Ideally, it should also be dry and sunny. In such conditions, *Heliohebe hulkeana* can form a very tight, compact bush. In cooler drier areas, exposure is not as essential.

PESTS AND PROBLEMS: If *Heliohebe hulkeana* shows sign of downy mildew, spray with a fungicide. Slugs find the leaves quite succulent, so watch for them — another advantage of a hot dry exposed site is that the slugs will not like it.

CARE AND MAINTENANCE: Like all hebes and hebe-like species *Heliohebe hulkeana* keeps a better form if pruned regularly, but if possible avoid pruning in late autumn and winter as this can lead to deformed new growth. Always prune after flowering, preferably before the plant begins seed production in the spent heads. *FACT TIME: If a plant is flowering excessively, it usually means it is under stress, e.g. too wet or too dry, too exposed, or not the right amount of sunlight. If this is the case, the plant will put all its remaining energy into reproduction, as survival of the species is the most important thing. Hence, it will flower at the expense of vegetative growth, then seed, then die. This process can be stopped midstream; if a plant seems to be flowering more than usual, remove the flowering heads before they seed and relieve the stress. This may mean transplanting the plant.*

Some people believe *Heliohebe hulkeana* benefits from applications of lime but I have found that this makes little difference, as long as the soil conditions are appropriate to start with.

Heliohebe hulkeana is best propagated by cuttings, which root moderately easily.

LANDSCAPING SUGGESTIONS: *Heliohebe hulkeana* contrasts well with species of unusual form such as *Coprosma virescens* and *Carmichaelia arenaria* and can look equally good with herbaceous species such as Marlborough rock daisy and rengarenga. If conditions in the garden are not suitable, try growing *Heliohebe hulkeana* in a pot.

- Approximately 50 cm high and wide
- Full sun to semi-shade
- Dry conditions essential in humid areas
- Wind hardy
- Frost hardy
- Coastally hardy

Left: *Heliohebe hulkeana*

Below: *Hibiscus trionum*

Hibiscus trionum

There is debate about whether this species is native to New Zealand or was introduced by the Maori, and to add to the confusion a slightly different form occurs 'naturally' on Mercury Island. Some believe that this form, which has smaller flowers without the dark centre, is the true native *Hibiscus trionum*. *H. trionum* is a short-lived perennial herb that grows to about 40 cm in height. It has an attractive combination of fine dark stems and dissected dark green leaves, but the main feature is the flowers, which are 4–5 cm across, and pale yellow with a lovely dark purple centre. The plant begins flowering in spring, continuing through until autumn. Over this period there is nearly always one flower on the plant and sometimes 20 or more.

It is found naturally only in upper parts of the North Island in isolated coastal spots.

LIKES AND DISLIKES: *Hibiscus trionum* is tolerant of extremely dry conditions and in fact can thrive in them; the size of the bush is not affected, and flowering almost seems to be encouraged. Conversely, very wet and frosty conditions should be avoided. Exposure, even to coastal winds, is not a problem, and while it grows more densely in full sun, it will tolerate semi-shaded conditions.

PESTS AND PROBLEMS: There are no major pests or problems.

CARE AND MAINTENANCE: *Hibiscus trionum* responds extremely quickly and well to even very severe prunings. If the plant is looking stretched or you would like to reshape it, it is best to prune it back quite hard during or at the end of the flowering season.

The easiest method of propagation is by seed, although cuttings are also quite successful. *Hibiscus trionum* seeds quite readily and young plants will happily pop up around the parent.

LANDSCAPING SUGGESTIONS: This is a wonderfully floriferous small herbaceous shrub that is suitable for just about any garden. The prolific flowering, hardiness and seeding qualities of *Hibiscus trionum* make it ideal for a cottage garden, where it could be planted with *Linum*, *Helichrysum*, *Pimelea*, rengarenga and *Parahebe* species. It can even look good planted among cacti and succulents in a hot dry bed, adding a contrasting shape and form. In semi-shade it can become rather stretched, but this is not a problem if it can be supported by other species such as Chatham Island forget-me-not, *Adiantum hispidulum* and native grasses.

RELATED SPECIES: *Hibiscus diversifolius* is not at all like *H. trionum* in form but the flowers are very similar. It is a small bush that grows 1–2 m tall, although there is also a prostrate form. The leaves are not as dissected as those of *H. trionum* and are a spring green colour, and it has fine prickly bristles on the stems and leaves. *H. diversifolius* is frost tender.

- Perennial herb 40 cm tall
- Full sun to semi-shade
- Dry hardy
- Wind hardy
- Tolerates light frosts
- OK in coastal gardens

Ⓞioi is a fine, reed-like plant that occurs both in swamps and on the driest of rocky cliffs. In the former situation the 'reed' can be almost blue green in colour, while in the latter it can take on a lovely orangey hue. Oioi is slow spreading, has a wonderful erect yet weeping habit, and grows to 1.5 m in height. The reeds, which are 1–2 mm in diameter, are actually flowering stalks, and the leaves are

Flowering head of oioi

reduced to the little black lines that have given rise to the common name 'jointed rush'. It has separate male and female flowers that are both fairly insignificant, although when flowering the female plant takes on a lovely overall red hue.

Oioi occurs on the coast throughout New Zealand, in salt marshes and inland on marshy lakeshores in the central North Island.

LIKES AND DISLIKES: Oioi prefers full sun but will tolerate semi-shade. Exposure is not a problem and it will tolerate very dry to very wet conditions. A very hardy species.

PESTS AND PROBLEMS: There are no major pests or problems with this species.

CARE AND MAINTENANCE: The only maintenance that may be required is reducing the spread of the plant. If left unfed it will acquire a lovely orange hue.

It can be propagated by seed or division. When dividing make sure the pieces are not too small; 5 cm round is ideal.

LANDSCAPING SUGGESTIONS: Although oioi is considered a wetland species, it will grow quite happily in normal garden conditions. If the space available is limited, it can be planted in a large container dug into the ground. Oioi can be planted with dwarf flaxes, prostrate manuka, *Metrosideros perforata* 'Adult form' and *Acaena inermis* 'Purpurea', or it could be planted by a small water feature with parataniwha, *Polystichum vestitum*, kiokio and *Machaerina sinclairii*. For the natural look, plant it with cabbage trees, manuka, harakeke, *Carex secta* and *Gunnera prorepens*. Try it in a large pot, by itself or with *Heliohebe hulkeana* and *Pimelea prostrata*. Oioi has a wonderful fluid look and in the wind moves like a flowing river.

- 1–1.5 m tall
- Full sun to light shade
- Wet hardy
- Dry tolerant
- Wind hardy
- Frost tolerant
- Coastally hardy

Despite its common name this species does not look at all like an iris. At first glance it could be confused with a broad-leaved *Carex*, as the habit is the same. The flat blade-like leaves can attain a height of 50 cm, and the whole plant can have a similar width. The leaves may be soft and flexible or quite rigid, depending on where the plant is sourced from, but it is the flowers and seed pods that really distinguish this species. In spring, the flower spikes extend to nestle in among the leaves, just below the full height of the plant. The 3-petalled flowers are white and about 2 cm across, and the seed pods that appear after flowering are bright yellow. These pods can remain on the plant for months, occasionally not opening until the new flowers are set the following season.

Libertia ixioides can be found growing along stream margins and among rocks throughout New Zealand, from sea level to around 600 m.

Libertia ixioides

LIKES AND DISLIKES: Especially in warmer regions, *Libertia* prefers dry or free-draining sites. Exposure to sun and wind is not a problem, and it will even tolerate quite shady conditions.

PESTS AND PROBLEMS: The correct moisture levels must be maintained, and the soft-leaved form can be susceptible to snail and/or slug attack.

CARE AND MAINTENANCE: The old leaves can be pulled out if desired, but when doing this hold the plant firmly at the base so that you do not pull out pieces of plant; it is not a deep-rooting species. When mulching and composting ensure the base of the plant is left clear; make a doughnut with the plant in the hole.

Both division and seed propagation are viable options. In both cases, make sure the potting medium does not become too wet, which can encourage fungal growth in the soil and above it. If dividing a plant, reduce its bulk by cutting the leaves to at least half their original size; this minimises stress, as the plant has less leaf matter to maintain with its reduced root system. When propagating with seed watch for slugs and snails.

LANDSCAPING SUGGESTIONS: *Libertia* can provide contrasting colour and form in a large planting of native grasses, and it is excellent in exposed situations with species like the Marlborough rock daisy, hebes and *Sophora* 'Dragon's Gold'. It makes a good filler under established vegetation, whether native or exotic, and its contained habit makes it ideal for rockeries. In a shaded rockery *Libertia ixioides* can be planted with ground ferns such as *Asplenium oblongifolium*, *Blechnum pennamarina* and *B. novaezelandiae*, providing a contrast in form. In the sun it could be planted with *Corokia cotoneaster*, mountain totara, *Metrosideros perforata* and *Acaena inermis* 'Purpurea'.

SIMILAR SPECIES: *Libertia grandiflora* grows to the same height as *L. ixioides* and the foliage is virtually identical, but the flowerheads extend above the foliage and the seed capsules are black and open almost immediately after ripening.

Libertia peregrinans

Libertia ixioides 'Creeping Form' is exactly as its name suggests, with stiff pale green leaves not unlike those of *L. peregrinans* in form.

Libertia peregrinans has a very erect, spiky habit and slowly spreads through underground rhizomes. The leaves can be almost copper coloured in full sun, the margins having the strongest, almost orange, coloration. If growing vigorously or in the shade, the plant may be almost green but as the growth slows the orange colour becomes more evident.

- Herb 50 cm high, 50 cm wide
- Full sun to shade
- Dry tolerant
- Wind hardy
- Frost hardy

Linum monogynum forms a small bush that will grow to 40–50 cm in height. If left unpruned it tends to be quite lax as the upper branches are fine; if shaped regularly it can form a lovely open bush. It has attractive leaves that are quite soft, linear and blue green in colour, but it is the white flowers that are the main feature. These are up to 3 cm in diameter and smatter the plant from spring through to early autumn. The plant tends to be quite short lived but it seeds readily.

Linum monogynum occurs throughout New Zealand in dunes and rocky places from the coast to around 600 m.

Flowers of *Linum monogynum*

LIKES AND DISLIKES: *Linum monogynum* is tolerant of very dry situations but will be more luxuriant if planted in a good free-draining loam. Damp sites should be avoided. In shade, the plant will tend to become more open in its form.

PESTS AND PROBLEMS: The only potential problem is its prolific seeding, but any unwanted plants are easily weeded out.

CARE AND MAINTENANCE: The only maintenance required is regular pruning to shape the bush. For the first 6 months, or even a year, be brave, ignore the flowers and concentrate on pruning — it will be worth it in the long run!

There are no problems with propagation; the plant will do it by itself!

LANDSCAPING SUGGESTIONS: The superb flowering habit of *Linum monogynum* makes it a wonderful addition to any garden. A magnificent specimen plant can be created as a feature in a rockery or open space, or it could be planted with other dry-loving species like *Podocarpus nivalis*, rengarenga, small-growing flax cultivars and *Chionochloa flavicans*. As always, remember to plant the taller-growing plants where they will not shade the smaller ones. *Linum monogynum* is ideal in a cottage garden and can also be planted in a container, either by itself or with groundcovers like *Acaena inermis* 'Purpurea' or *Muehlenbeckia axillaris*.

- Herb 40–50 cm
- Full sun to semi-shade
- Tolerant of dry conditions
- Wet intolerant
- Wind hardy
- Frost tolerant
- OK in coastal gardens

CULTIVARS: *Linum monogynum* 'Innocence' is a very low-growing form that has a spread of about 30 cm. It forms a very dense mound, with the white flowers extending above.

This species looks more like an iris than a sedge. The dark glossy green foliage forms from the centre of the plant and is thick and tussock-like. It varies from 30 cm to 1 m in height and is at least as wide. The flowering heads extend above the foliage and form lovely drooping panicles of a rusty brown colour in spring. These heads stay on the plant through summer as the seeds mature. This is a magnificent sedge that is underutilised in New Zealand gardens.

Machaerina sinclairii in full flower

It occurs naturally from North Cape to around the Tararua Ranges, from sea level to 450 m.

LIKES AND DISLIKES: In warm areas *Machaerina* prefers a cool root run, and when planted in full sun a drier, more free-draining soil, as it can be prone to root rot. If planted in shade, or in cooler parts of the country, it will tolerate quite wet conditions. Exposure is not a problem.

PESTS AND PROBLEMS: If conditions are too wet, the fungus will show through a blackening of the leaves. This can generally be dealt with by spraying with fungicide, but move the plant if the problem persists. If it becomes stressed through excessive moisture or dryness, the leaves can become spotty or deformed; alleviate the problem and the deformities will disappear.

CARE AND MAINTENANCE: The old leaves and flowering stems can be cut off if you prefer a tidy-looking plant. If removing the flowering stems, remove the leaves surrounding them at the same time, as they will die off anyway.

Machaerina can be propagated by division, but make sure the pieces are not too small. Seed is easier if large numbers are required.

LANDSCAPING SUGGESTIONS: A large planting of *Machaerina* can look quite striking, especially among *Olearia lineata*, *Astelia banksii* and *Muehlenbeckia astonii*. It can also be planted in a mixed garden planting with *Sophora* 'Dragon's Gold', *Chionochloa flavicans*, rengarenga, *Coprosma rhamnoides* and *Blechnum pennamarina*. If planted in a shady part of a rock garden it could be a mock Poor Knights lily, as the foliage of the two is very similar.

- Tussock grass 30 cm–1 m
- Full sun to shade
- Dry tolerant
- Wet tolerant in cooler areas
- Wind tolerant
- Frost tolerant

Chatham Island forget-me-not is a striking plant — a herb that looks lush and tropical yet comes from a very exposed southern region. The leaves are a glossy green and can be up to 30 cm in diameter. The plant itself can stand 60 cm high and be at least as wide. Although the foliage is magnificent, it is the flowerheads, which form in late spring, that tempt most people. These are 10–15 cm in diameter and normally a vivid blue, although there are now selected forms of both pink and white. The reason there is not a plant in every garden is that they are notoriously difficult to grow!

As the common name suggests this species is native to the Chatham Islands, where it can be found on sandy beaches and rocky outcrops.

LIKES AND DISLIKES: Chatham Island forget-me-not does not like high humidity or moist sites, as it is very prone to fungal attack from *Phytophthora* and black spot. In areas with high humidity it is best to find a spot that is exposed to the prevailing winds and either very free-draining, sheltered from the rain (e.g. under the eave of a roof) or under well-established vegetation. Shade is not a necessity as long as the root system can be kept cool; large rocks are ideal for this. In cooler climates, free-draining soil is the most important factor. No matter where it is Chatham Island forget-me-not likes a rich soil.

PESTS AND PROBLEMS: Slugs and snails find the lush, fleshy leaves of the Chatham Island

The lush foliage and flowers of Chatham Island forget-me-not

forget-me-not irresistible. If the plant is showing signs of black spot or the leaf stalks are starting to blacken at the base, spray it promptly with a fungicide, or a combined fungicide-insecticide which will also relieve the slug and snail problem, at least for a period. Keep an eye on the plant for a few weeks to ensure some plant vigour is returning. If there is no sign of new growth, cut it back hard and transplant it to a drier area or a planter.

CARE AND MAINTENANCE:

In the right situation virtually no care and maintenance is needed apart from the occasional wary eye for slug/snail damage. A good feed, preferably high in nitrogen, should be given once or twice a year; the leaves will start to yellow if the plant needs feeding. If the site is not ideal, you will need to keep an eye out for fungal problems. Some people believe that regular doses of sea water give a healthier plant.

Seed is the main way of propagating Chatham Island forget-me-not, although the plant will bulk from the base and can be divided.

White-flowering Chatham Island forget-me-not

LANDSCAPING SUGGESTIONS: If you do not have the right spot in your garden, I suggest you don't waste your money, although you could try it as a pot plant. On the coast it could be planted with *Pachystegia*, *Astelia banksii*, *Geranium traversii*, kowhai and whau, or it could be planted underneath a specimen tree with *Adiantum hispidulum*, *Festuca coxii* and rengarenga with *Pimelea prostrata* on the edge. In an exposed rockery it can look wonderful on its own, just nestled in among the rocks.

- Herb up to 60 cm tall
- Full sun to shade
- Wet intolerant
- Wind hardy
- Frost hardy
- Coastally hardy

The Marlborough rock daisy is another plant that is ideal for those very dry exposed areas where nothing else will grow. It has large, leathery grey-green leaves on fine grey branchlets, all of which are covered in a fine tomentum. In spring the plant starts to form relatively large flower buds that extend above the foliage like drumsticks. The soft grey buds sit there for what seems a long time then eventually open into lovely white daisy flowers with yellow centres. The plant itself can grow to over a metre across and at least 50 cm in height, but not overnight!

Marlborough rock daisy

Pachystegia occurs naturally along the Kaikoura and north Canterbury coastlines and inland to the central mountains. It is most commonly found on very exposed, harsh sites, often in areas with apparently no soil, from rocky outcrops in the sea off Kaikoura to steep mountainous inland areas.

LIKES AND DISLIKES: *Pachystegia* handles conditions that are usually the domain of succulents, and should be treated similarly — do not water! A northerly aspect is ideal, maximising sunlight levels and dryness. Light shade is fine but will result in a shrub with a more open habit and larger leaves.

PESTS AND PROBLEMS: Fungal attack is of major concern in areas of high humidity so plant in as dry a site as possible. If you don't have a suitable site, try growing *Pachystegia* in a pot; to prevent moisture levels becoming too high, especially in winter, do not put a tray under the planter. Keep the watering to an absolute minimum.

CARE AND MAINTENANCE: *Pachystegia* is virtually maintenance free. If the plant becomes too large for its site, just prune it back; it buds away again freely from the base of the plant. If *Pachystegia* becomes too shaded, it will lose its habit and become stretched as it tries to find higher light levels; if the plants growing around it begin to shade it, prune them back.

Seed is the easiest means of propagation. The downy seedhead that forms after flowering can easily be removed when the seeds are ready for sowing. Make sure you don't over-water the seed tray; like the adult plant, the seedlings are very prone to fungal attack. *TIP TIME: A good general rule when sowing seed is to cover the seed to the same depth as the size of the seed. For example, if the seed is 3 mm thick cover it with 3 mm of soil. If, like* Pachystegia, *the seed is very fine, you can sprinkle it over the tray and just water it in. If you prefer covering your seed, use a very fine sieve and just do a light dusting over the top.*

Mature plant of Marlborough rock daisy

LANDSCAPING: Its low maintenance and tolerance of extreme dryness make *Pachystegia* a must for exposed gardens. Since it likes similar conditions, it does not look out of place growing among succulents and cacti. Its bold grey foliage also contrasts well with *Carex*, *Heliohebe*, Chatham Island forget-me-not and herbaceous groundcovers such as *Acaena inermis* 'Purpurea' and *Helichrysum bellidioides*. *Pachystegia* is excellent planted at the base of an established border where the older, larger plants will naturally use most of the moisture. On the coast it could be planted with flaxes, taupata, *Metrosideros perforata*, *Coprosma acerosa* and *Chionochloa flavicans*. Always make sure *Pachystegia* has adequate light levels.

SIMILAR SPECIES: *Pachystegia rufa* is very similar to *P. insignis* but the grey foliage has a delicate bronze hue, especially on the underside.

Pachystegia minor is also very similar but has smaller darker green leaves, and is smaller overall and more compact. I have found it to be a hardier species in the Auckland region. It is ideal for small rock gardens.

- Herb 50 cm tall, 1 m wide
- Full sun or part shade
- Dry site essential
- Wind hardy
- Frost hardy
- Coastally hardy

This cultivar is a selected form of *Parahebe cattaractae*. It has relatively large dark green serrated leaves, 20–30 mm x 10–15 mm, and grows to a height of 30 cm. *Parahebe* 'Snowcap' is a slow-spreading herb, which spreads not only from its base but also from stems that fall to the ground and root at the point of contact. Its height and leaf size make it a little unusual for a parahebe but give it more presence in a garden situation. The white flowers are formed on flowering spikes that extend above the foliage. Flowering begins in spring and can continue through to autumn.

LIKES AND DISLIKES: In general, the more shade a parahebe has the more lax and open the plant; in full sun it will be much tighter in its form. Exposure also causes the habit to tighten. Parahebes do better in free-draining soil, and as long as the moisture regime is kept under control it is quite a hardy species.

PESTS AND PROBLEMS: In humid areas, high moisture levels can be lethal as parahebes are very susceptible to root rot. They are also prone to powdery mildew and black spot, both of which can be sprayed for with a fungicide. These problems can be minimised by planting in an exposed position.

CARE AND MAINTENANCE: To maintain a tight habit it is advisable to prune the plant after flowering, to at least half its height, forcing the development of new shoots. It is best to do this

Parahebe 'Snowcap' in flower

while the plant is still growing quite vigorously; if it is done in winter, the new shoots may be deformed through fungal problems, and the plant can take many months to recover. In northern areas *Parahebe* 'Snowcap' may benefit from being cut back twice a year as growth tends to be more vigorous and the growing season longer.

Parahebe species are easily propagated by cuttings.

Parahebe hookeriana

LANDSCAPING SUGGESTIONS: *Parahebe* 'Snowcap' is a relatively low-growing herb that can look excellent in a rock garden, on the coast, in a border planting, a stony path, or even a mixed cottage garden. In a rock garden it could be planted with *Festuca coxii*, dwarf flaxes, Marlborough rock daisy and *Geranium traversii*. On the coast it could be nestled in among astelias, Poor Knights lily, Marlborough rock daisy, rengarenga and *Coprosma acerosa* 'Red Rocks'. It is also effective in a hanging basket with *Pimelea prostrata* or in a planter with *Astelia banksii*.

SIMILAR SPECIES: *Parahebe catarractae* is slightly smaller-growing than *P*. 'Snowcap' and not as floriferous. It occurs naturally on rocky cliffs near streams and waterfalls.

Parahebe decora forms a sprawling mat. Its small leaves are deep green above and reddish below, and in summer it has mauve to white flowers. It occurs naturally east of the main divide from Marlborough to Southland.

Parahebe hookeriana has small bristly oval leaves and mauve flowers in summer. It occurs naturally in subalpine to alpine regions of the Central Plateau.

Parahebe lyallii is a variable species that grows to about 20 cm and has a slightly sprawling habit. The rounded, toothed leaves can have a reddish tinge. The small flowers are white to pink and are borne on flowering spikes up to 8 cm long. *Parahebe* 'Blue Boy' is a selected form with 'blue' flowers in spring and summer, and there is also a selected pink form. It occurs in mountain areas throughout the South Island.

- Herb 20–30 cm tall
- Full sun to semi-shade
- Dry tolerant
- Wet intolerant in humid areas
- Wind tolerant
- Frost tolerant
- OK in coastal gardens with some shelter

The common name of this species of flax is misleading, as *Phormium cookianum* commonly occurs on the coast throughout New Zealand as well as on high country. It has two quite distinct forms: an erect plant that grows to between 60 cm and 1 m tall, and a larger weeping form that grows to 1–1.5 m. The flower stalks of both form in spring and tend to stand above the foliage. The bright yellow flowers are followed by a twisted, drooping seed pod. Nectar-feeding birds love flax flowers and can be seen landing on a flower stalk and slowly working their way from top to bottom.

LIKES AND DISLIKES: Mountain flax is not as tolerant of wet conditions as

Phormium cookianum 'Green Dwarf' in flower

its relative harakeke, especially in areas of high humidity. It is, however, very tolerant of dry conditions and salt-laden winds. It prefers full sun but will tolerate light shade. In deeper shade the plant becomes very open and lax in its form.

PESTS AND PROBLEMS: The pure species of flax do not have many disease problems but some of the cultivars can be difficult to keep clean. It helps to plant the flax in a moderately exposed position, and do not let the plant get too wet or too dry. The juvenile

Phormium tenax (harakeke) flowers

plants, and the young leaves, can be susceptible to slug damage, which can cause holes or runnels in the leaves. If the plant has white encrusted patches on the underside of the leaves, it probably has a type of scale; this can be dealt with by spraying with summer oil and a contact insecticide. For brown leaf spots, remove the worst-affected leaves, then spray with copper oxychloride.

CARE AND MAINTENANCE: *Phormium cookianum* requires virtually no maintenance; the old leaves can be removed if so desired.

Phormium 'Platts Black'

LANDSCAPING SUGGESTIONS: The pure species of flax are quite large but can be contained by cutting off the outside leaf clusters. The weeping form of *Phormium cookianum* takes up more room than its erect counterpart, even if it is cut back, but if you have the space it is a spectacular plant. The more erect, generally lower-growing form is ideal for even the smallest of gardens and can even be grown in a planter. The classic look is to plant mountain flax with cabbage trees, *Coprosma rhamnoides* and assorted *Carex* species, but it can also be planted as the main feature, combining *Brachyglottis*, Marlborough rock daisy and prostrate manuka with it. On the coast it could be planted with taupata, *Coprosma acerosa*, oioi, *Astelia* rengarenga and *Carex testacea*. *Phormium cookianum* is useful in providing protection for more delicate plants as it is fast growing and tolerates a high degree of exposure. For the same reasons, it can be planted as a low-growing hedge.

Phormium 'Sundowner'

SIMILAR SPECIES: *Phormium tenax* (harakeke) is a very hardy species that grows a lot taller than *P. cookianum*, reaching 2 m or more, and is commonly more erect in its habit. The 3–5 cm long flowers are a lovely dull red and occur on flowering spikes that can be 3–5 m tall. The leaves are dark green. In areas where both species occur together *Phormium cookianum* tends to flower before *P. tenax*, minimising hybridisation.

PHORMIUM CULTIVARS BY LEAF COLOUR:
Almost all the cultivars prefer dry situations, especially in humid areas, as they are prone to root rot. For some species, like *Phormium* 'Platt's Black', dry conditions are essential. A good general rule of thumb is to keep to exposed and

Phormium 'Cream Delight'

dry sites; foliar diseases are less common in exposed areas. The variegated species can revert to a single colour; to prevent this, cut out the reverted clump.

Apricot tones
up to 1 m:
'Apricot Queen' (E)

1–1.5 m:
'Sunset' (E)

Red/dark pink/bronze
up to 1 m:
'Evening Glow' (W)
'Pink Panther' (W)*
'Rainbow Surprise'

1–1.5 m:
'Rainbow Queen' (E) *
'Rainbow Maiden' (W)*

1.5–2+ m:
'Firebird' (E)
'Guardsman' (E)*
'Sundowner' (E)*

Bronze/purple/black
up to 1 m:
'Bronze Baby' (E)*
'Chocolate Fingers' (E)
'Jack Spratt' (E)*
'Platt's Black' (W)
'Rubrum' (W)
'Thumbelina' (W)
'Tom Thumb' (E)

1–1.5 m:
P. cookianum 'Bronze' (W)*
'Dark Delight' (W)

1.5–2+ m:
P. tenax 'Bronze' (E)*
'Black Prince' (W)
'Burgundy'

Cream/yellow & green
up to 1 m:
'Duet' (E)
'Gold Sword' (E)

1–1.5 m:
'Cream Delight' (W)
'Goldspike' (E)
'Tricolor' (W)
'Yellow Breaker' (E)
'Yellow Wave' (W)

1.5–2+ m:
'Radiance' (W)
P. Williamsii 'Variegata' [[okay?]]

Green
up to 1 m:
'Elfin' (E)
'Green Dwarf' (E)*
'Greensleeves' (W)*
'Surfer' (E)*

KEY: (E) = erect habit; (W) = weeping habit; * = hardy.

This species can take 15 years to flower, but it is worth the wait. The bright green leaves are not unlike a large iris in shape and size; they stand quite erect, only arching when grown in light shade or very sheltered conditions. The Poor Knights lily is not unlike an orchid in that after a number of years the most floriferous plants tend to be the ones that are a little root bound. The dark red flowers occur on tall flowering stems that extend above the leaves, which can be up to 1 m long. The flower spikes tend to lie perpendicular to the flowering stems, with all the bottle-brush-like flowers facing upward. These flowers form in spring and are quite spectacular.

Xeronema occurs naturally only on Poor Knights Island and Hen Island in the Hauraki Gulf.

Poor Knights lily in flower

LIKES AND DISLIKES:
Xeronema has three major dislikes: water, deep shade and frost. It requires very, very dry or free-draining soil, and is unaffected by exposure, coastal or otherwise.

PESTS AND PROBLEMS: Moisture is the major problem as *Xeronema* is very susceptible to fungus, both above and below ground. If there is any blackening of the base of the leaves or excessive yellowing of a well-fed plant, spray with a systemic fungicide and alleviate the moisture problem, if necessary transplant. Yellow spots can also form on the leaves, and this is generally a sign of too much water. The plant will grow out of the problem once the stress has been alleviated.

CARE AND MAINTENANCE: If planted in the right spot, *Xeronema* can be virtually maintenance free, just requiring the occasional feed. If using compost or mulch, make sure they are kept well away from the base of the plant. Some people are staunch believers in placing seaweed around the base, and seaweed is good plant food but difficult for people living inland to get.

Xeronema can be propagated by division, but do not break it into pieces that are too small. For bulk production seed is used, but it can be difficult to germinate and it is very slow growing for the first few years of its life.

LANDSCAPING SUGGESTIONS: The need for dryness greatly limits the potential of *Xeronema* in the garden. In areas with high rainfall plant it under the eave of a roof or on the sunny side of well-established trees that will suck most of the moisture out of the ground. In clay soils you could also try building up a garden, putting in a lot of large rocks for the roots to wander through. Add Chatham Island forget-me-not, *Pachystegia*, *Heliohebe hulkeana* and *Festuca coxii*. *Xeronema* is completely happy on a frost-free coast, where it could be planted with *Coprosma acerosa*, rengarenga, *Chionochloa* and *Astelia* species, ensuring that the latter will not shade the *Xeronema* too much while it is establishing. If there are no suitable sites in the garden, *Xeronema* makes a wonderful pot plant. It requires virtually no watering, although if the leaves do look a little flaccid, pour water over the plant and leave it to recover. A north- or west-facing deck is ideal, but lift the plant off the ground if the surface it is sitting on is not porous; do not use a tray under the plant! Do not pot it into too big a pot, as spare soil holds moisture; since *Xeronema* is very slow growing it will not use up the moisture very quickly and will be sitting in a damp environment. A root-bound plant will also flower more quickly and more prolifically.

> - Large herb up to 1 m tall
> - Full sun to light
>   shade
> - Needs dry conditions
> - Wet intolerant
> - Wind hardy
> - Frost tender
> - Coastally hardy

Adiantum hispidulum is aptly named rosy maidenhair as the new fronds have a lovely apricot to quite pink hue to them; this colour is stronger the more light there is. Not many species keep their pink or red coloration in light shade as this species does, so in this situation it adds a spot of colour to the normal green of the undergrowth. Like most maidenhair species it spreads slowly and is not vigorous in its growth. The fern frond consists of the 'stalk' and the lamina (the 'leaf'); the 'stalk' of the rosy maidenhair is very fine and black, 30–40 cm tall. On top of this sits the very thin, dissected, olive green lamina, up to 35 cm long x 30 cm wide.

This species of maidenhair occurs naturally throughout the upper half of the North Island and in localised pockets further south, through both islands.

LIKES AND DISLIKES: Rosy maidenhair prefers a shady, sheltered site with dry, free-draining soil, but it will tolerate full sun as long as it is not exposed. It is intolerant of wet conditions. Surprisingly, with its thin fronds, rosy maidenhair will tolerate light frosts.

PESTS AND PROBLEMS: There are no major pests or problems with rosy maidenhair.

CARE AND MAINTENANCE: If the plant becomes too wet the new fronds will wilt and the underground rhizomes will start to rot. If this occurs, dig the fern up and move it to a drier location. Spray it with a fungicide if you think this is necessary. Apart from that little maintenance is necessary, although the old fronds can be cut off if desired.

Propagation can be by spore, a job for a specialist or at least an enthusiast, or by division. The divisions should be 4–5 cm in diameter.

LANDSCAPING SUGGESTIONS: As it can withstand high light levels this is an ideal fern to use under open-canopied trees like kowhai, ngaio or whau. In such situations it could be planted on its own or with *Libertia* species, Chatham Island forget-me-nots and other ground ferns. The delicate foliage will add softness to any planting. It can be slotted in under establishing puka or pukanui, the fronds slowly creeping into the light as the fern grows. *Asplenium oblongifolium*, with its glossy green simple fronds, is an excellent complementary fern to plant with it, providing a contrast to the more finely dissected fronds of the maidenhair. If the garden is too wet or exposed, rosy maidenhair will do just as well in a pot.

SIMILAR SPECIES: *Adiantum aethiopicum* is the smallest of the native species. The bright green fronds are more finely divided than *A. hispidulum* and the plant can form a dense groundcover. As with exotic maidenhairs, the plant can be trimmed close to ground level and it will burst into life again.

- Fern approximately 50 cm tall
- Shortly creeping
- Full sun to shade
- Prefers dry or free-draining conditions
- Wind intolerant
- Tolerates light frosts

One of New Zealand's best-known tufted ferns, this was probably one of the first ground ferns to be brought into cultivation, as much for its ease of cultivation as for its beauty. The common name hen and chicken fern comes from the small plantlets or 'baby ferns' that can form on the margins of the old fronds. When the old fronds collapse the young plants root into the soil on which they have fallen. A fully grown hen and chicken fern can have fronds over a metre in length, forming an impressive structure in the undergrowth. These fronds can vary in their dissection from moderately simple to almost lace-like, depending on where the plants were sourced from.

Asplenium bulbiferum is common throughout New Zealand in lowland to lower montane forests.

Plantlets on a hen and chicken fern frond

Mass planting of hen and chicken fern

LIKES AND DISLIKES: Like a lot of *Asplenium* species *A. bulbiferum* does not like waterlogged or wet soil, especially in warmer areas. It prefers a moist rich free-draining growing medium, although it will tolerate moderately dry conditions. It will tolerate full sun as long as the situation is not too exposed, but the fronds will become a yellow-green colour as opposed to the dark green of plants grown in the shade.

PESTS AND PROBLEMS: The major pests are slugs and snails, which especially attack the fresh young fronds. If left unattended for a long time, these pests will keep eating the new fronds until the plant has used up all its reserves and the plant slowly dies.

CARE AND MAINTENANCE: Keep a wary eye out for slug damage and treat accordingly. A yellowing of the fronds indicates one of three possibilities: that the light levels are quite high, that the fern could benefit from feeding, or that the ground is too wet. Check these out and deal with them accordingly. When feeding ferns remember to keep the crown of the fern clear, and if using granulated fertiliser, keep it off the fronds as it may burn them.

To propagate the fern you can place the plantlets on propagating medium and new plants will develop. Cut the small plants off the parent frond, ensuring that some of the frond is still attached. Spore can also be used, but this is a specialised operation.

LANDSCAPING SUGGESTIONS: Hen and chicken fern can act as a filler under established or establishing vegetation as the trees start to develop trunks, leaving a clear space underneath. It has a softness that *Asplenium oblongifolium* does not have, although the two can contrast with each other in a planting, the hen and chicken fern in the moister hollows and *A. oblongifolium* on drier raised areas. It can also be planted with kawakawa, *Astelia banksii*, kiokio and other ground ferns, and native grasses. There is no reason why hen and chicken fern cannot be planted under a deciduous or semi-deciduous tree; the more yellow coloration that the fronds will take on in the light will create a seasonal change in the look of the garden. As a pot plant, hen and chicken fern can live for many years in a cool shaded room with only minimal maintenance — the occasional foliar feed, a wary eye for house-plant diseases (commonly mealy bug, scale and red spider mite) and occasional repotting into new soil to give it a new lease on life.

- Tufted fern up to 1 m high
- Prefers light shade to shade
- Tolerates full sun
- Prefers moist, free-draining soil
- Prefers shelter

Asplenium oblongifolium has bold, shiny green fronds that are quite simple in their form. It is one of New Zealand's more striking species, tropical and lush in appearance. Over time the fronds can reach over a metre in length and will form a clump of a similar width, but it is not a fast-growing species. It is the perfect species to plant under established vegetation where it is dry and shady.

It occurs naturally throughout the North Island and as far south as Banks Peninsula on the east coast of the South Island and Greymouth on the west. It grows from the coast to lower montane forests.

LIKES AND DISLIKES: *Asplenium oblongifolium* prefers a very dry environment; in the wild it can be found perched on tree fern trunks, or in the fork of large old puriri. In very dry situations like these it will grow very slowly. It will tolerate full sun but the plants will tend to have much shorter, fleshier fronds and be a more yellow-green colour than if grown in the shade.

PESTS AND PROBLEMS: Slugs and snails are the main pests, first devouring the young fleshy shoots then moving on to the older leaves when these have all gone. Over time they can kill the plant, but the problem can be minimised if it is planted somewhere dry. In wet situations fungus is also a problem, another good reason to plant in the dry. Passion vine hoppers are attracted to

A lush clump of *Asplenium oblongifolium*

Asplenium oblongifolium, so keep a wary eye on the plant in areas where they are a problem and if necessary spray with an insecticide.

CARE AND MAINTENANCE: The main maintenance task is regular snail and slug patrol. Despite its preference for dry conditions *Asplenium oblongifolium* will still benefit from some composting and/or mulching; make sure the crown of the fern is left completely clear. The old fronds can be removed if you wish.

Asplenium oblongifolium is very difficult to propagate and it is really the job of an expert. It requires a moist, but not too moist, sterile environment for at least two years from the time the spore is spread on a tray. The little ferns take a long, long time to develop and continue to be very slow even once they are large enough to be handled.

LANDSCAPING SUGGESTIONS: *Asplenium oblongifolium* contrasts well with the small-leaved coprosmas that are often a feature of dry shade. It could also be planted with kawakawa and rengarenga, which like the same conditions and also require some slug and snail protection. You could also try planting *Asplenium oblongifolium* as an epiphyte. Take a small hanging basket, line it with sphagnum moss and plant in a small fern. The potting medium should have nutrients and natural moisture-holding capabilities, for example a mix of compost, topsoil and friable clay. Ideally, leave the fern for about six months to settle into its new soil medium, then remove it from the hanging basket and tie the sphagnum moss around the root ball to create a new container. This container can then be tied to a tree fern trunk, where it will slowly root into the trunk, or it can be perched in the crook of a branch. If you want to try growing *Asplenium oblongifolium* in exposed conditions, it is best to place the fern, in its pot, in the open air for at least a month to harden off before planting it out. *Asplenium oblongifolium* is also excellent as an indoor pot plant.

- Tufted fern 1 m+ high
- 1 m+ wide
- Prefers semi-shade to shade
- Dry hardy
- Wet intolerant
- Wind tolerant

The common name crown fern is an appropriate one as the fronds of this fern form in a circle around the centre of the plant and are quite upright in their habit, creating a crown-like appearance. The yellow-green to dark-green fronds are simply dissected and can be up to 1 m long x 15 cm wide. Like all species of *Blechnum*, the crown fern has separate fertile fronds that stand quite erect in the centre of the plant. These begin forming in autumn and stay on the plant through to spring when the new sterile 'normal' fronds form. A mature plant can actually form a small stocky 'trunk' 50 cm or more tall, lifting the plant even higher off the ground. It can also form short runners and spread in that way, although very slowly.

In the wild, crown fern is found throughout New Zealand in coastal to montane forests. At times dense thickets of it exist, especially in disturbed areas.

LIKES AND DISLIKES: This is a very easy species of fern to grow. The perfect conditions are a rich moist free-draining soil in a sheltered position, but it will tolerate a wide range of conditions — full sun through to shade, a degree of wind exposure and moderately dry conditions. In warm areas it is better in drier conditions rather than wet as it can be prone to root rot.

PESTS AND PROBLEMS: There are no major pests or problems with crown fern.

CARE AND MAINTENANCE: Very little maintenance is required. The old fronds can be cut off if you like, as can the old fertile fronds at the end of winter. Mulching will help maintain soil moisture; it does not matter if mulch comes in contact with the trunk of a mature plant, but make sure the crown is left clear. It is a species that transplants moderately easily, and any new plants that form through spreading or sporing can be dug up and moved; just reduce the frond height by at least half.

For propagation details see *Blechnum novae-zelandiae*.

LANDSCAPING SUGGESTIONS: Crown fern is an ideal species of fern to plant under a deciduous tree. The winter exposure will cause the foliage to yellow a little, but apart from that it will be fine. It could be planted with *Libertia*, rengarenga, *Hebe diosmifolia* and *Carex* species. Alternatively, a large bed of crown fern could be planted with the occasional group of *Coprosma rhamnoides* and kawakawa. A mixed planting with *Carex dissita* and *Fuchsia procumbens* is also effective. If planting in the sun, select a sheltered position as the fronds can become wind burnt. In such situations it could be planted with divaricating plants like weeping mapou and *Muehlenbeckia astonii*, and with mountain totara and *Blechnum pennamarina* as groundcovers.

- Tufted ground fern approximately 1 metre tall
- Full sun to shade
- Prefers shelter
- Dry tolerant
- Frost tolerant

The shuttlecock shape of crown fern

Pink-hued new fronds of kiokio

Blechnum novae-zelandiae, syn. *Blechnum 'capense'* • KIOKIO

Kiokio is a very variable fern, ranging in size from only 30 cm to nearly a metre in height and width. The size variation occurs in different regions as well as different growing conditions. One of the many wonderful things about kiokio is the pink hue the new fronds take on if exposed to sunlight. It is also very hardy, handling not only very wet situations but also very dry, and tolerating both full sun and deep shade. In fact, kiokio will grow just about anywhere. It will soften boundaries between sunny and shady areas, grow under decks, under shrubberies, and even survive on the coast although it will tend to be smaller. The fronds are up to 30 cm wide and simple in their form, while the 'leaflets' often have slightly wavy margins.

Kiokio is one of New Zealand's most common ferns, occurring throughout the country from the coast to the mountains, and from swamps to hard dry banks.

LIKES AND DISLIKES: If kiokio is planted in a site that is extreme environmentally, for example dries out excessively or is very exposed, it may take a season to adapt. When planting in such areas it is best to plant smaller plants and/or plants that have been sourced from a similar environment; they may be better suited genetically to the conditions.

CARE AND MAINTENANCE: In late autumn and winter kiokio will often have black patches on its fronds and occasionally they will be almost completely black; this is not a sign of ill health. Around this time the growth rate of most species slows down considerably as they prepare for the winter months ahead. The black patches seem to be part of this preparation. Do not cut the leaves off, but let the plant undertake its natural seasonal course. When new frond growth appears in spring the older, blotchy fronds can be cut if desired. The dead brown fronds can be cut off whenever you like. If kiokio is planted in a very dry spot its fronds may wilt or, in a worst-case scenario, die off completely. First, don't panic! Next, check the centre of the fern where the new, unfurled fronds lie; if the centre is hard the fern is still alive (so water it well), if it is mushy, the fern is dead. *TIP TIME: checking the crown of a fern to see if it is firm is the easiest way to tell if a sick-looking fern is alive or not.*

As with most ferns, propagation is a fickle business. The easiest method of bulking numbers is to leave the area around a plant undisturbed for a year or two, keeping it moist and as sheltered as possible. These conditions will allow the fern spores to develop into young ferns, which can eventually be planted out.

LANDSCAPING SUGGESTIONS: Kiokio will look its grandest in a sheltered, semi-shaded, moist environment, but it will tolerate just about any situation. To enhance the pink hue of the new fronds plant the fern where it will receive some sunlight, direct, filtered or reflected. Don't assume this fern must be planted in a fernery — kiokio can be planted among herbaceous plants, providing a contrast in form, or under a border planting where it is often too dry for other species. Exposed south-facing banks are equally possible, as are planters.

- 30 cm–1 m in height and width
- Full sun or shade
- Tolerates wet or dry soil
- Tolerates poor soil
- Wind hardy
- Tolerates light frosts

*B*lechnum pennamarina is easy to grow and very hardy. It is a low-growing groundcover that is suitable for both sunny and shady sites; if it is exposed to some sunlight, reflected or otherwise, the new growth takes on a lovely pink hue. In full sun *Blechnum pennamarina* will hug the ground but in more shaded situations the fronds can grow to 20 cm high x 2 cm wide. The fronds are simply dissected and almost linear in form. Like other *Blechnum* species *B. pennamarina* has separate fertile fronds that are much finer than the more prominent sterile fronds. The colour of the fronds can range from yellow green in full sun to a quite deep green in the shade. *B. pennamarina* occurs naturally throughout New Zealand from dry grassland to forest margins.

Fronds of *Blechnum pennamarina*

LIKES AND DISLIKES: *Blechnum pennamarina* prefers drier rather than wetter conditions but is generally very hardy; an easy fern to grow.

PESTS AND PROBLEMS: The hardiness of this fern is confirmed by its lack of real problems or pests.

CARE AND MAINTENANCE: As *Blechnum pennamarina* is moderately slow growing you don't have to worry about it dominating a planting. To maximise growth mulch and/or compost regularly.

The easiest method of propagation is by division, but make sure that each piece is of a reasonable size (at least that of a 50-cent piece) and that it has roots. Spore can also be used but requires more patience and the right conditions.

LANDSCAPING SUGGESTIONS: *Blechnum pennamarina* can be planted just about anywhere in a garden. I tend to favour areas of high light where the pink colour of the new fronds is accentuated. Its non-invasive nature means it can be planted with other low-growing species such as *Libertia* or dwarf flaxes. It can look equally good as a groundcover, meandering through other ferns and shade-loving species. It is also effective when planted among rocks, either in a rock garden or around a water feature.

- Groundcover
- 5–10 cm high
- Full sun to shade
- Tolerates dry conditions
- Wind hardy
- Frost hardy

This is another hardy species, as demonstrated by its survival in areas destroyed by fire and its persistence after an area has been logged. The dark green fronds commonly grow to 1 m long x 20 cm wide, although they can grow up to 1.5 m long. The fronds are quite harsh in texture with sharply toothed margins. It is a slow-growing species, but over time *Polystichum* will form a small, stocky 'trunk' of about 20 cm in diameter and take on the appearance of a miniature tree fern.

Polystichum vestitum

However, even before it forms a trunk *Polystichum vestitum* has a lovely habit. The long new fronds tend to stand quite erect; in time they are pushed to the outside by the next batch of new fronds. The dead leaves remain attached to the plant for a long time and can form a skirt around its base.

Polystichum vestitum occurs naturally from the Auckland isthmus south throughout the rest of New Zealand. Its habitat tends to be lowland to montane forests.

LIKES AND DISLIKES: *Polystichum vestitum* is best suited to a moist shady site, either on the southern side of a building or under existing vegetation. In light shade it will tend to be a little shorter but still very healthy. It will tolerate full sun, although the normally dark green fronds will tend to become more yellow green in colour. In very windy and/or dry conditions the tips and margins of the fronds can become burnt, especially on the new fronds.

PESTS AND PROBLEMS: The main pest is thrips, which can be controlled with an insecticide. Occasionally, if the plant is growing in a still, humid area, it can be susceptible to fungal attack, manifested in a wilting of the new fronds. Use a fungicide if this occurs.

CARE AND MAINTENANCE: The old brown fronds can be removed, but apart from this *Polystichum vestitum* is maintenance free. A good mulch or compost will be welcome from time to time, but make sure the crown of the fern is not covered as this can kill it.

LANDSCAPING SUGGESTIONS: Suitable low-growing species to plant with it are *Carex dissita*, *Blechnum pennamarina*, *Libertia ixioides*, and groundcovers such as *Fuchsia procumbens* and *Mazus radicans*. *Polystichum vestitum* is also a good species to plant on a margin between a sunny and a shady site, being tolerant of both conditions.

- 1 m high
- Full sun to shade
- Tolerates dry and wet conditions
- Tolerates some wind
- Frost hardy

Purple piripiri is a vigorous, hardy herbaceous groundcover of the Rosaceae family. It is a purple-leaved form of the less commonly cultivated grey-leaved *Acaena inermis*. To attain the best colour, with the fine feathery foliage hugging the ground, plant in full sun. If planted in light shade the leaves can attain a height of around 5 cm, and the colour will shift to a grey purple. *FACT TIME: most plants with red or purple in their foliage will attain their best colour if planted in full sun; i.e. more sun, more colour.*

Piripiri has a moderate growth rate, and a single plant can have a spread of a metre or more.

Acaena inermis occurs most commonly on gravelly riverbeds and tussock grasslands on the eastern side of the South Island and sporadically elsewhere .

LIKES AND DISLIKES: Good drainage is beneficial; in areas prone to high humidity, moderately dry or free-draining conditions are essential. Piripiri will also tolerate and even thrive in exposed situations where other species will fall by the wayside.

PESTS AND PROBLEMS: If high moisture or humidity levels exist for too long, it can lead to dieback from fungal attack.

CARE AND MAINTENANCE: If you wish to keep it contained, piripiri can be maintained with simple trimming and weeding out from around the margins. Unwanted weeds will still come

Acaena inermis 'Purpurea'

up within the mat formed by the piripiri but this is not a major problem. *TIP TIME: when weeding in mat-forming groundcovers, use an old screwdriver to penetrate down where the main root of the weed is, lever it, then pull out the whole weed intact. This minimises disturbance to the groundcover and ensures you remove the whole weed, roots and all.*

When to feed piripiri? If it is planted in full sun, it will start to lose its bright colour when it needs feeding. Plants in light shade will also fade and lose vigour.

Seedheads of *Acaena microphylla*

If piripiri becomes too dry, the exposed leaves can die off, but water it well and it will recover. The dead leaves will become quite crisp and can be removed with just a good brush with your hand.

Division is by far the easiest way to propagate piripiri. Just dig out a piece of an existing plant, ensuring you have some roots and as much soil as possible, then replant and keep moist for a few weeks. Piripiri will also grow from cuttings but will take a little longer to establish. In either case it is best to do it when the plant is growing vigorously.

LANDSCAPING SUGGESTIONS: The wonderful thing about piripiri is that it is not an invasive groundcover but is still very hardy. It is excellent in rockeries, on its own or next to grey- or blue-foliaged plants; in fact there are very few plants with which it clashes. Because it can handle quite dry, gravelly situations it can also be planted among rocks or paving stones to create a softer edge. It can also be used as a groundcover for potted plants.

SIMILAR SPECIES: *Acaena caesiiglauca* is a very striking blue-green colour, almost turquoise. It does not bush readily and can form long runners if not tipped. It requires very free-draining or dry conditions, especially in areas prone to high humidity.

Acaena fissisitipula is blue grey in colour and more vigorous and hardier than *A. caesiiglauca.*

Acaena microphylla can be a moderately insignificant groundcover until the spiny seedheads form in summer. These stand well above the plant and are a striking red colour and, unlike most species of piripiri, the spines are not hooked so will not adhere to your socks! There is not only the standard bright green-foliaged form of this species but also one with attractive bronze leaves; both forms provide a dense cover.

- Groundcover
- Approximately 1 m spread
- Full sun or light shade
- Purple colour
- Dry tolerant
- Wind tolerant
- Will tolerate poor soils
- OK coastally

Some coprosmas are pure species and some are cultivars, but they all act as woody groundcovers. In general they are not dense enough to prevent weeds coming through, but they do minimise them. The best species for this are those like *Coprosma taiko* or *C. neglecta*, i.e. those with a dense habit. Some species will droop down retaining walls, e.g. *C. neglecta*, while others will keep mounding on top of one another until they almost form a long low bush, e.g. *C*. 'Prostrata'.

Coprosma acerosa spilling over a low wall

LIKES AND DISLIKES: Groundcover coprosmas all have a tighter habit in full sun, though they will tolerate semi-shade. They all thrive in average soil moisture conditions and some will tolerate it very dry. None will tolerate it very wet. Exposure is not a problem and generally nor is frost.

PESTS AND PROBLEMS: These species and cultivars tend to be disease and problem free.

CARE AND MAINTENANCE: Some forms are almost maintenance free, but others may require pruning to keep a good tight habit, especially if they are planted in light shade. When feeding groundcover coprosmas use fine compost and shake the plant so that it will fall through to the ground below. This will help keep the plant very healthy.

The main form of propagation is cuttings, which tend to root moderately easily.

LANDSCAPING SUGGESTIONS: In addition to being used as groundcovers, coprosmas can be espaliered or made into standards. To form an espalier, plant your coprosma at the base of a wall and, as it grows, attach it to the wall so that it is spread-eagled vertically. You can also shape it with judicious pruning. Species like *C*. 'Prostrata', *C. kirkii* and its cultivars, or even *C. acerosa* 'Hawera' can be trained in this way. Another option is to form standards out of them and let the foliage hang like open umbrellas; *C. neglecta* would be good for this.

SPECIES AND CULTIVARS:
• *Coprosma acerosa* (sand coprosma) has small fine soft green leaves on fine orange branches. It can form a springy mound and is very hardy coastally. The bush has an orangey hue to it,

touched with green The female plant has white berries.

• *Coprosma acerosa* 'Hawera' lies very flat to the ground unless planted in light shade. The branches lie in one plane, like a feather. It can be quite a dense groundcover.

• *Coprosma acerosa* 'Red Rocks' has fine dark leaves that are relatively insignificant. Its colour comes from its dark red-brown branches. It is springy like pure *C. acerosa*.

• *Coprosma* 'Black Cloud' has small dark green leaves rimmed with black, 15 mm long x 5–7 mm wide. They are tightly grouped on the plant, creating a dark green mat. As the plant's growth slows through autumn the leaves start to change, becoming more black than green; in winter they are almost completely dark, with no green. As spring approaches and growth resumes the colour shifts the other way.

• *Coprosma brunnea* is very similar to *C. acerosa* 'Red Rocks' but the branches are almost black. The female plants have lovely blue berries.

Coprosma neglecta

• *Coprosma* x *kirkii* is one of the most commonly used species of *Coprosma*. Its leaves are 10–12 mm x 5 mm and mid-green in colour. It can form a mound up to 50 cm tall x 1.5 m wide. The side branches can be quite far apart and the main runners very strong; to achieve a good habit it is best to prune it regularly. It is very vigorous.

• *Coprosma* x *kirkii* 'Goldstream' is very similar to *C.* x *kirkii* but has very golden branches and slightly longer but narrower leaves that are bright green. It is denser in its habit and has an overall golden/orange hue. It is also very vigorous.

• *Coprosma* x *kirkii* 'Variegata' is the same as *C.* x *kirkii* but has variegated leaves, sage green with a cream edging.

• *Coprosma neglecta* is interesting. The dull green leaves are almost round (5–10 mm in diameter) and nearly overlap one another. The branches curve downward, creating a mounding effect, the branches lying one on top of the other while still growing outward. It is capable of layering itself down a retaining wall for 40 cm or so. This species needs virtually no pruning to maintain it but is moderately slow growing.

• *Coprosma* 'Prostrata' is similar to *C. neglecta* in that the branches curve downward to create a mound. It can form mounds up to 1 m high, although it can easily be kept quite prostrate. The small glossy dark green leaves are oblong and about 10 mm long.

• *Coprosma* 'Taiko' has small dark green leaves and a very tight habit. It requires minimal, if any, pruning to keep a good habit.

> • Woody groundcovers
> • Full sun to semi-shade
> • Dry tolerant
> • Wind tolerant
> • Frost tolerant

Parataniwha is a herbaceous groundcover that is ideal for average to quite wet sites in the shade. The stocky, succulent stems run both above and below ground. In light shade the plant lies very flat to the ground; in the depths of the forest it becomes taller and more upright. In a moist, dark gully it can become well over a metre tall and develop a woody base. The leaves are made up of a number of leaflets that are quite rough and wrinkled with serrated edges. They are olive green, and in higher light levels have purple tonings. The insignificant flowers are borne on 'lumps' that look very like herbaceous galls.

Parataniwha occurs only in the North Island, as far south as the Tararua Ranges. It is found in damp shaded areas in lowland to montane forest. In some areas it can be the dominant groundcover.

Foliage of parataniwha

LIKES AND DISLIKES: If conditions become too dry, parataniwha will wilt and eventually, if these conditions persist, die. It prefers sheltered shady conditions and is tolerant of only very light frosts.

PESTS AND PROBLEMS: Parataniwha is prone to slug and snail damage.

CARE AND MAINTENANCE: Parataniwha is not too vigorous so can easily be kept under control. Make sure the plant does not dry out.

The easiest method of propagation is cuttings, which root very quickly and easily.

LANDSCAPING SUGGESTIONS: The leaf colour is one of the major attractions of this species, especially if it has a little filtered light, which accentuates the purple tonings. In light shade it forms quite a dense groundcover and could be used effectively with *Polystichum vestitum*, crown fern, kiokio, and *Carex* species. It is ideal for planting in a dark hollow on the southern side of a property where very little else will grow; plant it with tree and ground ferns, horopito, makamaka and putaputaweta. You will need to be sure the site is wet all year round. Full sun will cause the leaves to yellow a little.

- Groundcover low lying to 1 m tall
- Light shade to shade
- Dry intolerant
- Wet tolerant
- Sheltered conditions
- Tolerant of only very light frosts

This species is a very hardy groundcover which is quite happy to wander through an existing planting. It will not tolerate very harsh frosts, however. The soft green leaves, about 1 cm in diameter, lie flat to the ground unless it is in a very shady situation where the stems and leaves can stand slightly erect. The tubular flowers are quite large, around 2 cm in length, but not immediately obvious. The flowers are a yellow-orange colour, not strikingly different from the leaves, but the deep purple-red anthers are much more obvious and quite beautiful. The pinkish red berries that form after flowering are conspicuously large for the size of the plant. Flowering begins in late spring and continues through summer to early autumn, while berries continue to form through to early winter.

Fuchsia procumbens occurs naturally on the coast from North Cape to the Coromandel.

LIKES AND DISLIKES: Unusually, *Fuchsia procumbens* is so 'coastal' that it will tolerate the occasional wash with seawater and yet still withstand light frosts. The growth rate tends to be slower in full sun than light shade, and the foliage colour will tend towards yellow green. Although *F. procumbens* will wilt if it becomes too dry, it can easily be revived with a good soaking, unless it has been very dry for a long period. For optimum growth, plant in light shade in a rich free-draining soil.

PESTS AND PROBLEMS: *Fuchsia procumbens* is problem free.

CARE AND MAINTENANCE: If conditions are ideal for growth, this species can send out long runners that will need to be cut back if a more contained plant is required. It can look wonderful uncontained, meandering through the more upright vegetation around it. Occasionally it will climb over and through small plants, but it can easily be pulled out.

Fuchsia procumbens roots very readily from cuttings, the most common form of propagation, but seed could also be sown.

LANDSCAPING SUGGESTIONS: The wiry stems of *Fuchsia procumbens* support it when it cascades down a wall or over the side of a pot, situations where the flowers and berries are even more obvious. It can be a vigorous groundcover if conditions are right, so to reduce maintenance plant it where it can have a free rein. Groundcovers like this prevent wind and sun drying the soil, and once well established will reduce weed growth by shading the soil. In harsher conditions, e.g. in full sun, exposed situations, or poor soils, *Fuchsia* is more contained. It is excellent planted in a stony path or courtyard, where it can provide a softening look, or among large boulders in a rockery or around a water feature.

- Groundcover
- Full sun to semi-shade
- Tolerates moderately dry conditions
- Coastal

CULTIVARS: *Fuchsia procumbens* 'Variegata' has a pale grey leaf with a creamy white margin. The berry tends to be pink, rather than red. It can provide an unusual contrast to other foliage in a shady situation.

Fuchsia procumbens foliage and flowers

Gunnera prorepens showing
bright red fruiting spikes

Gunnera prorepens

Unlike many exotic *Gunnera* species, New Zealand's are very small in stature. *G. prorepens* has unusual bronze to purplish green foliage that hugs the ground. The leaves are oblong and about 2 cm long. Although *Gunnera* occurs naturally in quite damp or wet areas, it is equally happy in soils of average moisture. The most striking feature of *G. prorepens* is not its flowers but the bright red berries that form in summer through to autumn. The small berries stand above the foliage on small spikes up to 10 cm tall. This species has separate male and female plants, so if you want the berries, ensure that you purchase a female plant.

Gunnera prorepens occurs from the Waikato southwards in damp spots within forests, grasslands and alpine herbfields in lowland to subalpine areas.

LIKES AND DISLIKES: In dry or frosty conditions the upper leaves have a tendency to die off, although the plant will only die if the conditions are extreme, as the lower rhizomes, which can remain unharmed, will burst into life when the conditions are right. If grown in semi-shade, the leaves tend to stand erect on their petioles, while in full sun they lie flat.

PESTS AND PROBLEMS: The only major problem is drying out, although if the plant becomes stressed, small discolorations may form on the leaves. If this happens, ensure the ground is moist, and feed.

CARE AND MAINTENANCE: *Gunnera prorepens* is virtually maintenance free. It can be contained by simply trimming and weeding out, although the stolons (stems that creep along the ground) are sometimes underground and need to be removed. It grows best in a well-fertilised soil, so feed regularly and keep moist.

Division is the easiest method of propagation. If rooted pieces are unavailable, a segment of stem can be partially buried, ensuring the nodes (where the leaves attach to the plant) are covered. Keep moist but do not over-water.

LANDSCAPING SUGGESTIONS: *Gunnera prorepens* can be used to create a natural margin along the edge of a pond, winding its way through *Carex secta* and flaxes. If planted in a hanging pot and watered regularly, it will cascade over the side.

> - Groundcover
> - Wide spreading
> - Full sun to semi-shade
> - Wet hardy
> - Moderately wind tolerant
> - Tolerates light frost

This is a species that should be planted in every rock garden. It has a slightly mounding habit and small pale green leaves that are grey on the underside, but the *piéce de résistance* is the small, white everlasting daisy-like flowers. These can form in late spring through to early autumn and stand above the foliage on delicate stalks about 5 cm long. The overall spread of the plant is about a metre.

Helichrysum bellidioides occurs from around the central North Island southwards. Its natural habitat is grasslands and open shrubland from lower montane areas through to subalpine.

LIKES AND DISLIKES: *Helichrysum bellidioides* prefers a sunny site but will tolerate semi-shaded conditions, although its habit will not be as tight. Avoid wet sites. Exposure is not a problem.

PESTS AND PROBLEMS: This species is not affected by any real problems or pests, as long as it is not too shady or too wet.

CARE AND MAINTENANCE: If your plant is becoming too large or too open in its habit, it can be pruned back. No fancy pruning techniques are needed, just cut! If it is starting to lose its vigour, feed it well and it will recover quite quickly.

H. bellidioides can root on contact with the ground, but if larger numbers are required the easiest methods of propagation are cuttings and division.

LANDSCAPING SUGGESTIONS: As it prefers quite high light levels *H. bellidioides* is good as a border plant, adding a soft margin to an open area, path or paved courtyard. In a rockery it can be planted on its own or as part of a larger planting with *Linum monogynum*, astelias, corokias and native grasses like *Carex buchananii*.

• Groundcover
• Full sun to semi-shade
• Dry tolerant
• Wet intolerant
• Wind tolerant
• Frost hardy

Flowers and foliage of *Helichrysum bellidioides*

Leptinella minor with its small button flowers

*L*eptinella minor is one of the few native species that can be used for a lawn (it has even been used as turf for lawn bowls). It has a lovely vivid green colour and the leaves are delicate and dissected like a fern frond. If it is planted in full sun, the leaves lie flat to the ground; if it is slightly shady, they will tend to stand more erect and be fluffier looking. The very small yellow button-like flowers that form in summer do not always have an immediate impact, but they are worthy of closer inspection.

Unlike many *Leptinella*, this species is found from North Cape south through both islands. It occurs naturally on the margins of swamps and streamsides, and on sandy tidal flats.

LIKES AND DISLIKES: *Leptinella minor* prefers free-draining soil that is neither too dry nor too wet. If planted in the wet in warm humid areas, it can be susceptible to root rot; if the soil is too dry, it will wilt and may die back a little, although parts of it will recover unless it has been too dry for too long. Exposure is not a problem as long as there is moisture available.

PESTS AND PROBLEMS: The only problem is keeping the moisture level correct. There are no real pest problems.

CARE AND MAINTENANCE: Its tight nature can make *Leptinella minor* difficult to feed, so make sure you plant it in a good rich soil that will sustain it for a few years. After the nutrients in the soil are used up it will become more yellow green, and it will be time to either foliar feed or sprinkle with granulated fertiliser. Compost is difficult to apply, although if you have fine loamy compost, it is by far the best thing to use. Sprinkle it lightly over the plant, making sure the leaves are not covered completely. If you want to reduce the plant's cover, just dig it out.

The easiest and most common method of propagation is division.

LANDSCAPING SUGGESTIONS: The fine feathery foliage creates a lovely soft look if *Leptinella minor* is planted underneath and/or around other plants, but remember that it requires some light. It could be planted with *Griselinia lucida* as the main feature plant, coming down to *Muehlenbeckia astonii* and *Carex buchananii*, with *L. minor* as the soft finishing touch. It can be used to soften the border of any planting or even rocks; try it among rocks around a water feature or meandering through a pebbly path. Then of course there is the lawn. This will take time to establish and it will need weeding, but it will not require mowing! *Leptinella minor* has an average growth rate, neither fast nor slow, so you will need a number of plants to form your lawn. For faster establishment plant in early spring. For a large lawn, you could buy your plants in autumn, bulk them up (by division) in a warm place through winter, then plant out in spring. When dividing the plants use a sharp gardening knife or a pair of old secateurs. A piece about 4 cm in diameter, or square, is perfectly adequate to plant. It is better to plant more smaller plants then fewer larger plants.

- Groundcover
- Full sun to semi-shade
- Wind tolerant in moist situations
- Frost hardy
- OK in moist coastal gardens

These are some of the few natives that will actually cascade down a wall, although in a rather stiff fashion. The foliage is pale green to silvery for the pink- and white-flowering forms, and dark bronze green for the red. They vary in height from ground-hugging to almost a metre in height, but they all have the same main outward, rather than upward, branching pattern. As they are cutting grown they will flower in their first year and all are quite floriferous, often flowering more than once a

Leptospermum 'White Cascade'

year, especially in areas with a long growing season. They are an excellent groundcover and easily maintained.

LIKES AND DISLIKES: *Leptospermum* are very tolerant of dry conditions and will also tolerate it moderately wet, although the growth rate will tend to be slower. In full sun they have a very tight habit, and they become more open the more shade they have, although some forms like *L.* 'White Cascade' still maintain a good habit with only half-day sun. Exposure is not a problem, in coastal or other areas.

PESTS AND PROBLEMS: See *Leptospermum scoparium*.

CARE AND MAINTENANCE: As for manuka shrubs, keep a wary eye out for diseases and treat accordingly. The prostrate manuka tend to respond faster and more readily to pruning than the shrub forms, possibly because the branches are lying exposed to the light. If a plant becomes very open and less vigorous, it is in need of sustenance; mulch and compost will both provide food and improve soil quality. Remember to keep both well away from the main stems of the plant.

LANDSCAPING SUGGESTIONS: *Leptospermum* can look wonderful woven in among other open species like *Euphorbia*, *Muehlenbeckia astonii* or kaka beak. *L.* 'Pink Cascade' and *L.* 'Red Falls' will do this best. I have seen *L.* 'Pink Cascade' growing in among oioi, the branches of the manuka woven in among the reeds, and the flowers looking almost as if they are suspended within the vegetation. Being woody, and therefore self-supporting, the prostrate manuka are ideal for planting at the top of a wall or steep bank, where they will fall outward and downward. If the fall is on a southerly aspect, the downward growth will tend to be less vigorous as the plant will naturally aim for areas with the highest light levels, which will not be down the wall, but if the aspect is right you can get a fall of 2 m or more. *Leptospermum* are also excellent in coastal gardens, and could be planted with flaxes, astelias, *Euphorbia*, *Brachyglottis*, grasses and even upright forms of manuka. If the upright forms match the groundcover in leaf and flower colour, the effect is of a single plant that is both prostrate and erect. Then there are the standard prostrate manuka. These can look quite spectacular, as the trunks tend to be a lot more gnarled than those of the shrubs and are quite clear once the standard has been formed. To achieve this choose a prostrate plant with a strong branch that can be pulled upright, stake it, trim off the lower side branches and let it grow. It will require regular restaking until the trunk has firmed. Prune the lower branches until the standard is the desired height then let it fill out.

CULTIVARS:
• *Leptospermum* 'Pink Cascade' has single pink flowers in spring and often again in autumn. Its habit is slightly upright at 60 cm–1 m, but it can have a spread of at least 2 m.
• *Leptospermum* 'Red Falls' has single deep red flowers in late winter and often again in late summer to autumn. It can also have a slightly upright yet spreading habit, at 1 m x 1–2 m.
• *Leptospermum* 'Wairere' has very light pink flowers in summer. It has a very tight habit and readily cascades.
• *Leptospermum* 'White Cascade' is similar to *L.* 'Wairere' but has white flowers in late spring and often again in autumn. Its foliage tends to be slightly greener than the grey of *Leptospermum* 'Wairere'. It also has a very weeping habit.

> • Woody groundcovers
> • Full sun to semi-shade
> • Dry tolerant
> • Wet tolerant
> • Wind hardy
> • Frost hardy
> • Coastally hardy

Mazus radicans

Unlike many groundcovers, *Mazus radicans* still hugs the ground even when planted in moderately deep shade. It is not an overly vigorous species but slowly creeps out into the available space. The leaves are a lovely bronze green colour with fine black markings which are only fully appreciated up close; they may remind you of a moth's wing in their delicacy. They average about 3 cm long x 1–2 cm wide, and tend to lie almost on top of one another. This is a species that

Mazus radicans in full flower

is most noticeable when it is in flower, although the flowers also require close examination to be fully appreciated. Up to 2.5 cm across, they are white with beautiful yellow and purple throats. They form in late spring and continue through summer.

Mazus radicans is found throughout the South Island and in the lower half of the North Island. It tends to occur in damp places at 150–1000 m.

LIKES AND DISLIKES: Although it occurs naturally in damp places, when growing it in the north of the North Island it is best to plant *Mazus radicans* in moist free-draining soil, as *Phytophthora* can become a problem in waterlogged soil. It will grow in full sun through to quite shaded conditions although it prefers a cool root run, which in warm areas can mean it is best suited to shaded sites.

PESTS AND PROBLEMS: Slugs and snails can be a problem. *Phytophthora* will show its presence through leaf loss and lack of attachment to the ground, as the roots will have rotted off. It will readily reroot from its nodes, however, so can be lifted and transferred to a drier location.

CARE AND MAINTENANCE: *Mazus* is one of those wonderful species that requires virtually no maintenance. If it becomes too extensive, dig it out at the boundary you want.

Division is the easiest method of propagation, although seed can be sown.

LANDSCAPING SUGGESTIONS: *Mazus radicans* is a lovely groundcover that is underutilised. It could be planted in a rockery in a cool hollow, in the shade under existing vegetation, or in the gravel of a shaded pathway where it will add texture and variety. It could also be used as a groundcover in a potted plant such as hen and chicken fern or *Carex secta*. Remember, it is not a vigorous grower so do not plant other groundcovers nearby that will overwhelm it.

- Herbaceous groundcover
- Full sun to shade
- Prefers moist but free-draining soil
- Wind tolerant
- Frost tolerant

*M*uehlenbeckia is an unusual genus in that it has groundcovers (*M. axillaris*), vigorous high-climbing vines (*M. australis*), low-climbing coastal vines (*M. complexa*) and shrubs (*M. astonii*). *M. axillaris* is not so vigorous that it will take over a garden, but if left to its own devices it can spread over some distance. In full sun it will either hug the ground or be a few centimetres tall, although some forms can grow as tall as 10 cm. The fine wiry branches do not provide much support and tend to lie along the ground, or even underground. Both the leaves and the flowers are very small, being dark green and white respectively. Although the flowers are very delicate they are not inconspicuous. Male and female flowers often occur on the same plant; after flowering the female flowers form small

Muehlenbeckia axillaris flowers and foliage

Muehlenbeckia axillaris as a groundcover beneath a mixed planting including lancewoods

opaque white fruit that actually taste quite nice.

Muehlenbeckia axillaris occurs naturally from the bottom half of the North Island southwards. It grows in gravelly and rocky places or in open grasslands, from the montane sector to the subalpine.

LIKES AND DISLIKES: *Muehlenbeckia axillaris* is really shown to its best in full sun or semi-shade; in more shady situations it has a very open habit. It is very tolerant of wind and dry situations but not wet.

PESTS AND PROBLEMS: *Muehlenbeckia axillaris* is really pest and problem free; just avoid the shade and the wet.

CARE AND MAINTENANCE: If you need to reduce the spread of *Muehlenbeckia axillaris*, use a spade to form a new edge and dig out the material that is not required. Compost or mulch can be spread over the top, but ensure that some foliage is still visible; the plant will regrow through it.

It can be propagated by division, cuttings or seed. If using seed, ensure there are no other species of *Muehlenbeckia* around as it does hybridise.

LANDSCAPING SUGGESTIONS: *Muehlenbeckia axillaris* can be difficult to dig out, so it is advisable to plant it where it can roam at will, remembering that it is moderately vigorous. It is an ideal groundcover in a contained garden and could be planted with species like *Myrsine divaricata*, *Chionochloa flavicans*, hebes and flax cultivars. Groundcovers like *M. axillaris* help to reduce moisture loss by acting as a screen between the soil and the sun and/or drying winds; plant it in an established garden where it will have minimal effect on existing plants, apart from enhancing their overall appearance with its dark green leaves and improving their growing environment.

- Groundcover
- 1–2 m+ spread
- Full sun to semi-shade
- Dry tolerant
- Wind tolerant
- OK coastally

The common name 'New Zealand daphne' is used very loosely and tends to cover all species of *Pimelea* found in New Zealand. *Pimelea prostrata* is a hardy plant that forms a prostrate groundcover of about a metre in diameter. It has delicate bluish leaves that can have red margins and in good growing conditions are very closely set, overall forming a dense mat. The branches tend to be quite slender but are woody in nature, which enables *P. prostrata* to support itself if planted in a position where it can cascade down a wall. In addition to its attractive foliage this species can also be covered in small white flowers from spring right through to early autumn.

Pimelea prostrata occurs naturally the length of New Zealand, from sandy coastal situations to rocky alpine sites.

LIKES AND DISLIKES: *Pimelea prostrata* prefers drier situations in full sun; while it

The abundant flowers of *Pimelea prostrata*

Pimelea prostrata cascading down a small retaining wall

will tolerate semi-shade, it will tend to be more open in its habit. It will tolerate very exposed conditions, where it will have a very tight habit and the growth rate will be reduced.

PESTS AND PROBLEMS: There are no major pests or problems; just avoid wet and/or shady sites.

CARE AND MAINTENANCE: If *Pimelea prostrata* becomes very, very dry, some of the branches can die off. If this happens, prune the plant and water it well — light surface watering will be of no benefit at all! *Pimelea prostrata* responds quickly to pruning, which can be done at any time. A thick layer of compost or mulch annually will improve plant vigour.

Cuttings are the most common form of propagation, although seed can be sown. The benefit of cuttings is that you will have a small plant after only a few months and it will flower in its first spring.

LANDSCAPING SUGGESTIONS: *Pimelea prostrata* is ideal for exposed coastal conditions where many other groundcovers will shrivel up. It could be planted with Chatham Island forget-me-not, Marlborough rock daisy, *Coprosma repens* and grasses such as *Carex testacea* and *Carex flagellifera* 'Green'. It is ideal for planting at the top of a retaining wall, where it will cascade down; a prostrate manuka can be added to provide contrasting texture. In a rockery *Pimelea prostrata* can be planted with just about anything, as long as it will not eventually become shaded. You could try it with *Heliohebe hulkeana*, a group of *Libertia*, and *Myrsine divaricata*. In a cottage-type garden it makes a good border with *Parahebe* 'Snowcap', *Hibiscus trionum*, *Linum monogynum* and rengarenga.

- Woody groundcover
- Spread of about 1 m
- Full sun to semi-shade
- Dry tolerant
- Wind hardy
- Coastally hardy

CULTIVARS: *Pimelea prostrata* 'Blue' is a selected form that has a tighter habit and has quite blue foliage.

FEEDING TIPS FOR GROUNDCOVERS

- Sprinkle a granular feed over the groundcover. If it is herbaceous, make sure the nitrogen levels of the granules are not too high, as this will cause fertiliser burns on the leaves. This is not as important for woody groundcovers as the granules can, and should, be knocked off the plant onto the soil below.
- Compost can also be used. For woody groundcovers and taller herbaceous plants sprinkle the compost over and shake the plant; the compost will fall through to the ground below. With mat-forming herbaceous groundcovers lightly cover the plant but make sure some foliage is still visible. The plant will slowly grow through the compost; do this in spring, summer or early autumn to ensure the plant is growing.
- Liquid foliar feed can also be used but most provide food for only a short period and are best used as a booster.

This species provides an unusual habit and form, as well as being easy to grow and low maintenance. The plants that are in cultivation tend to be the low-spreading forms, which have an almost Japanese look. Mountain totara can have a spread of a metre or more, although this will take time. The stout branches can become quite gnarled over time, and with some judicious pruning can be exposed in their full glory; the plant can become a garden sculpture. The foliage is not unlike that of an adult totara, rather than sharp and spiky like the juvenile plant. The colour varies from green to an olive brown, although the new growth has quite a beautiful grey-blue hue.

Mountain totara occurs naturally from around the Auckland isthmus south through both islands. Its habitat tends to be subalpine scrub and upper montane forests although in the colder southern areas it can occur in lowland forest.

LIKES AND DISLIKES: Mountain totara prefers to grow in full sun but will tolerate semi-shaded conditions, the habit then being a little more open. A rich free-draining soil will provide the most vigorous growth rate, but mountain totara will tolerate very dry conditions, and in such harsh conditions will form a wonderfully tight plant. Its low-growing, spreading habit and tough leaves make it ideal for exposed sites.

PESTS AND PROBLEMS: Mountain totara can be susceptible to *Phytophthora* if planted in a site that is too wet, especially in more humid areas. This will show as loss of new growth. If this

Mountain totara (foreground) with a grey-leaved hebe

occurs, prune the plant back, lift it and move it to a drier spot. It is advisable to spray it with a systemic fungicide as well, as this will help it recover. In warmer areas a cool root run will minimise stress. This can be achieved with rocks, grasses and/or groundcovers.

Close-up of a female mountain totara showing bright red fruit

CARE AND MAINTENANCE: Mulching and feeding will improve the plant's growth rate and general vigour, but if you want a more gnarled plant, do not make conditions too good. Mountain totara can be pruned, but it will take time to recover.

Propagation is by cuttings or seed, cuttings generally being the preferred method.

LANDSCAPING SUGGESTIONS: The form of mountain totara contrasts well with tussock-forming native grasses such as *Carex secta, Chionochloa flavicans* and *Carex buchananii*. Another option is to plant it with blue-grey species like *Festuca coxii* and *Pimelea prostrata*, which will enhance the blue of the new spring and summer growth. It can look equally good on its own as a specimen in a rock garden or as a pot plant. As a pot plant it could also be planted with a small grass, or a low-growing groundcover like *Acaena inermis* 'Purpurea'. The main thing to remember is that mountain totara is very, very slow growing, so plant taller or faster-growing species where they will not shade it.

- 50 cm–1 m high, 1–2 m wide
- Full sun to semi-shade
- Wind hardy
- Tolerates dry conditions
- Frost hardy
- Tolerant of coastal conditions

Panakenake is one of New Zealand's most popular native groundcovers. It is very fast growing, tolerates full sun to semi-shade, dry conditions to moderately wet, is wind tolerant, and has white flowers for a good six months of the year and purplish red berries through winter. Its only down side is that if it really likes its situation it can be very vigorous, almost weed-like. If conditions are quite harsh, however, it can be excellent. The small green serrated leaves can be quite fleshy in exposed conditions. The stems lie along the ground but will also climb over low-growing vegetation and grow underground. The flowers are about 1 cm long and are very abundant from spring through to autumn. The berries that form afterwards are of a similar size.

Panakenake occurs naturally in quite damp areas from sea level to around 1300 m throughout New Zealand.

LIKES AND DISLIKES: If the area is too shady, panakenake can become very stretched and the leaves far apart, rather than the tight mat that will form in full sun or even semi-shade. In very dry situations the growth rate will slow and it will have a much tighter habit. If conditions are too humid and moist, it can become susceptible to root rot and general dieback, but generally it is very hardy.

Panakenake flowers

PESTS AND PROBLEMS: The lack of pests and problems is what makes this species so popular.

CARE AND MAINTENANCE: If panakenake becomes low in nutrients it will lose vigour and become more of a yellow green. Feed it if this occurs. Apart from this the only maintenance will be control if you have planted it in a situation that it loves. To control it just dig it out, remembering that it also has stems underground.

By far the easiest method of propagation is division, although seed can also be used.

LANDSCAPING SUGGESTIONS: In warm areas it is better to make life for this species as hard as possible, which will reduce the maintenance necessary. A harsh, exposed environment is the most limiting, yet you will still have a plant that looks good. Other species that could be grown with it in such situations include *Astelia banksii*, rengarenga,

Bright pink berries of panakenake

flax cultivars, *Corokia* species and weeping mapou. In cooler environs it will not be as vigorous and will not tend to overpower other plants. The only areas to avoid are those that are too wet or too shady.

SIMILAR SPECIES: *Pratia macrodon* is very similar to *P. angulata* but has much fleshier leaves and stems. The fleshier leaves make it more prone to snail attack, but as it prefers drier, free-draining conditions this tends not to be a problem. The flowers can be pale yellow to white.

- Groundcover
- Wide spreading
- Full sun to semi-shade
- Dry tolerant
- Wind hardy
- Frost hardy

Rubus parvus is a prostrate species related to bush lawyer. The midrib on the underside of the leaves has a line of fine thorns. The single leaves can be up to 9 cm long and 5–20 mm wide but they tend to be shorter in very exposed or dry conditions. In winter these dark olive green leaves can develop almost purple tones. There are separate male and female plants; both have small white rose-like flowers in spring that are about 1 cm in diameter. The female plant follows the flowering with small raspberry-like fruit 1–2 cm in diameter.

Rubus x *barkeri* used as an edging

This species is found naturally only in the South Island, west of the main divide from Nelson to Westland. It tends to occur on riverbanks and in lowland forest.

LIKES AND DISLIKES: *Rubus parvus* is very hardy in cooler climates but in the far north can become susceptible to root rot and powdery mildew, especially in damp conditions. To avoid this problem plant it in a dry, sunny situation. Its tolerance to exposure is indicated by its natural occurrence on riverbanks.

PESTS AND PROBLEMS: This species is pest and problem free if wet sites are avoided.

CARE AND MAINTENANCE: *Rubus parvus* requires virtually no maintenance. It is not a vigorous groundcover can be kept in check with a spade or trowel.

Propagation can be by division, rooted bits, cuttings or seed.

LANDSCAPING SUGGESTIONS: This is an ideal species to plant in dry exposed situations where little else will survive; for example, bare banks, areas where there is little or no topsoil, or in gravel. It will not be vigorous, but it will grow. Both this species and *Rubus* x *barkeri* are also sometimes used as a living deterrent to people and animals. Remember it too when looking for a groundcover to grow where nothing else seems to survive.

SIMILAR SPECIES: *Rubus* x *barkeri* is a naturally occurring hybrid that is just as hardy as *R. parvus*. It is more vigorous, and has stems that can loop across the ground, so it is less ground-hugging. Its leaves are a similar shape but are trifoliate.

- Groundcover
- Full sun to light shade
- Tolerant of dry conditions
- Wind hardy
- Frost hardy

*S*cleranthus uniflorus is often referred to as a native moss, but neither it nor its very close relative *S. biflorus* are mosses. Both are flowering plants and they have identical habits. The mounding, ground-hugging habit of *Scleranthus* makes it easy to see why it is thought of as a moss. The main visible difference is that mosses prefer shade and *Scleranthus* full sun. *Scleranthus uniflorus* can have a spread of a metre or more. It is a bright spring green colour with very small flowers that are of no real consequence.

Spring green of *Scleranthus uniflorus*

    Scleranthus uniflorus occurs naturally in dry exposed areas of the South Island east of the main divide.

LIKES AND DISLIKES: To grow this species well it is necessary to have full sun, without which it will become very stretched and lose its characteristic tight habit. The right moisture levels are

Darker green of *Scleranthus biflorus*

also critical. If they are too high *Scleranthus* will be susceptible to fungal attack, and if too dry the plant will tend to die back. A free-draining planting medium is best.

PESTS AND PROBLEMS: Pests are not a problem but plant in full sun and do not let the moisture levels build up.

CARE AND MAINTENANCE: If *Scleranthus* browns off in the middle, simply pull out the brown pieces, then remove a rooted piece from the edge of the mound and replant it in the area that has been cleared. It will slowly regrow and fill in the space. To contain the spread of the plant just dig or cut out any excess plant material; it will continue to grow from the new margins created.

Division is the easiest way to propagate this species although seed can be sown. In both cases make sure you use a free-draining medium.

LANDSCAPING SUGGESTIONS: Its low nature and cultivation requirements restrict plantings of this species to more open sites such as rockeries. Its simple form also fits well into a Japanese-style garden. *Scleranthus* is happy in a pot, although it is best to have no tray. It could be planted on the coast with tangled low-growing coprosmas such as *Coprosma acerosa* and/or the grey-foliaged *Brachyglottis* species. When planting *Scleranthus* with taller-growing species ensure it is positioned in a place where it will not be shaded as the plants grow.

SIMILAR SPECIES: *Scleranthus biflorus* is very similar to *S. uniflorus* but is slightly taller in its habit and a darker green. As it is taller it is more prone to losing its tight form if the light levels are too low and will fall open. Apart from this its growing requirements are identical to that of *S. uniflorus*.

- Low-growing
  groundcover
- Spread of
  approximately 1 m
- Full sun to light shade
- Dry tolerant
- Frost hardy
- Coastally hardy

Selliera radicans forms a very tight mat, and until it flowers it can look like a short bright green grass. In some forms the small narrow leaves lie flat on the ground, while in others they can stand up to 4 cm or more tall. The small white flowers that form in late spring and continue through to autumn normally sit just above the foliage, their height dependent on the height of the leaves. *Selliera radicans* is a wonderful groundcover that has only become more widely available in the last few years, although in some parts of the country you may still have to hunt around for it.

In the wild, *Selliera* is found throughout New Zealand in damp sites from sea level to 1000 m. It can be found in areas that are sprayed with saltwater or awash with fresh water.

LIKES AND DISLIKES: Dampness is generally not a problem, although *Selliera* prefers a moist, free-draining soil. If it is too dry it will wilt, but it can rejuvenate if it is not left in this state for too long. In light shade the leaves will tend to be a little longer, and if the shade is too deep it will become very lank and sparse. *Selliera* is more tolerant of dry conditions in light shade.

PESTS AND PROBLEMS: This is a very easy species to grow and has no real pests or problems.

CARE AND MAINTENANCE: *Selliera* is not a vigorous groundcover so does not have to be

Selliera radicans forms a tight groundcover

Selliera in flower

GROUNDCOVERS • 191

regularly cut back. Any weeds that penetrate its tight mat can be killed by pouring over salted water; *Selliera* is entirely tolerant of saline solutions (but make sure there are no other plants around that may be affected by run-off or percolation).

The easiest form of propagation for *Selliera* is division.

LANDSCAPING SUGGESTIONS: The bright green of *Selliera* can look wonderful as a border plant for a cottage garden, underneath *Linum*, rengarenga and *Festuca coxii*, or among pebbles on a lightly shaded pathway or living area (but remember that it does not like very dry conditions). It has been tried as a no-mow lawn with variable success. It will require irrigation in dry areas and poor soils that do not hold the moisture in summer. Ideally it should be planted in a rich soil; some say this should be a mixture of topsoil, sand and compost, while others believe that friable clay should also be added. The result is a stunning-looking lawn that can be kept weed free, in the centre anyway, by pouring over saltwater. Try it first in a garden bed, and if you like it, start digging up that lawn! *Selliera* can also be planted on the margins of water features where it may dip some of its runners into the water. It could also be used as a groundcover for potted plants, where it will cascade a little over the side of the pot, softening the edges.

- Herbaceous groundcover
- Full sun to semi-shade
- Damp tolerant
- Dry intolerant
- Wind hardy
- Salt tolerant
- Coastally hardy

FURTHER READING

Allan, H.H., *Flora of New Zealand*, Vol. 1, Government Printer, Wellington, 1961

Brownsey, J. & Smith-Dodsworth, J.C., *New Zealand Ferns and Allied Plants*, Bateman, Auckland 1989

Cave, Y. & Paddison, V., *The Gardener's Encyclopaedia of New Zealand Native Plants*, Godwit, Auckland 1999

Crowe, Andrew, *A Field Guide to the Native Edible Plants of New Zealand*, Godwit, Auckland, 1997

Gabites, I. & Lucas, R., *The Native Garden*, Godwit, Auckland, 1998

Metcalf, L., *The Cultivation of New Zealand Native Grasses*, Godwit, Auckland, 1998

— *New Zealand Trees and Shrubs: A Comprehensive Guide to Cultivation and Identification*, Reed, Auckland, 2000

— *The Propagation of New Zealand Native Plants*, Godwit, Auckland, 1995

Moore, L. B., & Edgar, E., *Flora of New Zealand*, Vol. 2, Government Printer, Wellington, 1970

Wilson, H. & Galloway, T., *Small-leaved Shrubs of New Zealand*, Manuka Press, Christchurch 1993